Front Matters

Prerequisite Readings for the
Evangel School of Urban Church Planting

· ·

Edited by
Rev. Dr. Don L. Davis
Rev. Dr. Hank Voss

TUMI Press
3701 East Thirteenth Street North
Wichita, Kansas 67208

Front Matters: Prerequisite Readings for
the Evangel School of Urban Church Planting

The Urban Ministry Institute
3701 East 13th Street North
Wichita, KS 67208

ISBN: 978-1-62932-308-4

Published by TUMI Press
A division of World Impact, Inc.

The Urban Ministry Institute is a ministry of World Impact, Inc.

Table of Contents

Welcome Letter

Greetings in Christ, dear fellow laborers in the Gospel of Christ!

On behalf of all of us here at TUMI International, I welcome you in advance in your participation in the Evangel School of Urban Church Planting! Much thought, prayer, and preparation has been put into the School, in anticipation of your arrival, and we are truly excited about the potential this School gathering has for the planting of healthy new churches for Christ in untouched communities! Your involvement is both welcome and dear to us; we look forward to meeting you, and whether you act as dean, coach, or church planter, we know God will bless your efforts to contribute to planting a church in the place where God has called you.

Regardless of your role in the church planting process. we believe that you will need to do some reading and reflecting beforehand on concepts we will consider once you are here. Therefore, in preparation for your training here at Evangel, please read through carefully the following key pages taken from the resources you'll receive once you arrive at the Evangel School. These writings are targeted to help inform and orient you to the critical concepts, processes, assumptions, and overall vision and strategy of our Evangel training sessions. We are convinced that your careful and thoughtful consideration of these materials will readily outfit you for the rigorous and exciting times of reflection, prayer, and dialogue that await you, here at the School.

Church planting is truly one of the most important acts that God's people can engage in. The Church is central to the story and plan of God, and those privileged to plant congregations of the Lord are doubly blessed. Not only are we granted the grace to represent Christ in a community or neighborhood where he may not be known in any way, but also, and just as important, we get to bear witness to the amazing acts of grace and mercy God the Holy Spirit accomplishes through his servants – those faithful church planters who labor for him as he draws folk to the Lord. Whatever your role, you share in this honor and blessing. Yes, all of us who contribute to the process have the distinct opportunity to make our mark as we are used of the Lord to plant outposts of the Kingdom in new places for Christ.

Thanks in advance for your thorough preparation for the School. We are truly grateful for your partnership in the Gospel. Our sincere prayer is that the Lord will provide you with all the grace and wisdom you need to make your mark as you contribute in the exciting work of planting a new congregation for Christ in a neighborhood where he desperately needs to be known.

In anticipation of God's blessing,

Dr. Don L. Davis
Sr. Vice President, Church and Leadership Development, World Impact
Director, The Urban Ministry institute
Co-Dean, Evangel School of Urban Church Planting

World Impact's Strategy for Church Planting

Rev. Efrem Smith

Source:
Planting Churches among the City's Poor, Volume 1,
pp. 288-291

"Crowns of Beauty: the indigenous and urban church planting initiative of World Impact."

Church Planting Purpose

Striving to plant as many churches as possible among the various cultures represented by the urban poor, in all of our cities and beyond.

1. Credibility

- We are not a Para Church or Suburban Church coming into the city. We are an urban missions' organization with 40 plus years of incarnational, cross-cultural ministry experience.

- Multiple staff that has over 20 years of Church Planting experience.

- President and CEO, has extensive church planting, church planting training, and church planting design experience.

- Significant research has been done on urban church planting through TUMI

- We are unashamedly evangelical (Gospel, Christ, and Word-centered)

- We are an interdenominational organization.

2. Theology and Biblical Foundations

- Use Isaiah and Ezekiel to lift up significance of "Crowns of Beauty."

- Embracing the Entire Epic of the Bible- "People of the Story"

- Embracing the multi-ethnic, multicultural, urban, and liberating dynamic of the Bible.

- Engaging the Kingdom of God and *Christus Victor*.

- We are informed by the Great Tradition.

- Planting urban churches which function as communities of theology, worship, discipleship, and witness.

Source:
Planting Churches among the City's Poor, Volume 1, pp. 288-291

3. The Movement's Missional Design

- The overall church planting movement will be one which reflects a "Three-self" Missional Design (self-sustaining, self-reproducing, and self-governing).

- We plant churches with World Impact staff that transition to indigenous leadership and churches which begin with indigenous leadership.

- *The dynamics of our church planting movements will be known by shared spirituality, the ability to contextualize, and to create and sustain standardized practices and structures.*

4. Values

- "The best way to restore Christians to vibrant theology, worship, discipleship, and outreach is to recapture the Church's identity as a People of the Story, through a re-connection to the Church's Sacred Roots." (Pg. 151- *Jesus Cropped from the Picture* by Allsman)

- *Connecting the Great Tradition, The Urban Poor, and Urban Church Planting*

- We plant church associations, facilitate movements, and engage collaborative partnerships.

5. Principles

- P.L.A.N.T. Acrostic

- Indigenous Urban Leader Commitment

- Historic Commitment to the Urban Poor and to Cities

- A Missional (incarnational) Approach

- Honoring multi-ethnic, multicultural, ethnic specific, and first generation-immigrant focuses

- Planting churches with the existing urban church

6. Supplemental Initiatives

- Urban Church Associations (UCA's)

- World Impact Associates (WIA's)

- The Urban Ministry Institute (TUMI)

- SIAFU (Chapters and Leadership Homes)

Source:
Planting Churches among the City's Poor, Volume 1,
pp. 288-291

7. Three Expressions (all include assessing, training, chartering, and resourcing)

- House Church (20-50 people)

  Can be understood as a small store in a shopping mall. Needs the connections to other small churches to both survive and thrive. Can meet virtually anywhere and can operate with a small footprint with little to no financial burdens. Can focus on a specific block, housing development, or network of families. A strong discipleship focus of indigenous leadership development can take place in this smaller connected group.

- Community Church (60-150 people)

  Can be understood as a grocery or convenience store. Focuses on a particular geographic identity and proximity, highlighting both the affinity, connection, and unique context of the congregation and the surrounding community. Developed around a deep calling and connection to a particular neighborhood. Will need a semi-stable place to meet (park, community center, or school). Partnership with other community churches is important.

- Mother Church (200+ people)

  Can be understood as a Walmart Superstore or Super Target. A missionally directed congregation that leverages its capabilities and gifts to be a . . .

  - Center of compassion, mercy, and justice ministries,
  - Nurturing headquarters for planting new churches, and
  - Incubator of other effective ministries among the unreached urban poor.
  - Note that a more rooted facility would be needed within this expression.

8. Church Planting Framework

- Church Planting School (Events, Training, Resources)
- A unified assessment, training, resourcing, and standardization strategy.
- Training World Impact Staff as coaches, mentors, and co-pastors.
- Assessing call and gifts of World Impact Staff/Indigenous Leaders. (school, assessment, charter)
- Partnerships (local churches, denominations and organizations)

Source:
*Planting Churches
among the City's
Poor, Volume 1,*
pp. 288-291

9. Delivery and Support

- Charter Budget-$15,000-$75,000 per church over 3 years and based on location/expression

- History and Current State- 72 churches planted and 45 active

- Goal: Plant 300 churches over the next 7 years (Cost: $15 million, Initial injection of $1 million)

- Target both C-1 and C-2 leaders.

- ***Church Resources Division will provide general oversight and Regions will implement.***

- ***Staff Needs – Begin with National Director, reporting to Don Davis and providing resourcing support to RVP's and EDM's.***

- Fund development strategy – National Planting Fund – split between regions with administrative percent, Regional Partnering Churches, and Regional Operating Budgets

- Factor in costs of Coaching, Church Plant in a Box ($100), Training, etc.

- Include Member Care as needed.

- Coaching and Mentoring Tools (Prepare, Work, and Review)

- Potential Goal Management Tool (Goal Span-Jeff Hunt)

- ***Set Chartering Goals in the areas of Theology, Worship, Discipleship, and Witness.***

Preface
How to Use This Guidebook

Source:
Ripe for Harvest,
pp. 11-22

The Evangel School of Urban Church Planting:
Boot Camp for Urban Church Planters

For more than forty years, World Impact has been dedicated to honoring and glorifying God and delighting in him among the unchurched urban poor by knowing him and making him known. An inner-city missions organization, our vision is to recruit, empower, and release urban leaders who will plant churches and launch indigenous church planting movements. We are convinced that God almighty desires to empower the urban poor to advance God's Kingdom in every city in America and beyond through the local church. Indeed, we believe that the Church's proclamation and demonstration of the Gospel is at the heart of God's kingdom mission.

Our *Evangel School of Urban Church Planting* trains and equips coaches, church planters, and church plant teams to plant healthy churches among the city's poor. In order to thrive in their efforts, urban church planters must adopt a clear theological vision and choose sound, culturally sensitive models and expressions of the church. They must apply biblical wisdom in order to effectively evangelize, equip, and empower unreached city folk to respond to the love of Christ, and take their place in representing Christ's Kingdom where they live and work.

This guidebook, the official text of the *Evangel School*, outlines a process of church planting that respects the unique cultures, environments, communities, and situations reflected in urban America. The PLANT approach outlined here provides practically wise and spiritually vital instruction to ensure that urban church planting teams will neither fail nor blunder as they seek to engage needy yet spiritually ripe unreached neighborhoods. The guidebook will guide teams through that process, with a focus on prayer, reflection, and wisdom to find God's unique call on each planter and team.

Filled with devotionals, seminars, exercises, and worksheets, with dozens of graphics, diagrams, and articles, this rich resource will empower church planting teams to design a strategy that will prove empowering to them. It can enable them to draft a course that is consistent with the vision God has given them to plant a healthy, Kingdom-declaring church, and launch movements that display the justice of the Kingdom among the oppressed. We are excited about both the interest and activity of many churches and denominations to establish outposts of the Kingdom

Source:
Ripe for Harvest,
pp. 11-22

in the neediest communities in our nation. Our prayer is that this resource contributes to that vision.

Church Planting – a Work of the Holy Spirit

Church planting is a spiritual activity. It is not like building a house or starting a business. It requires prayer, worship, fasting, teaching, discipline, and wisdom. Without the leading and provision of the Holy Spirit, we cannot possibly see a church planted among an unreached people group needing to know of the love of Christ. Knowing this, the objective of this book is to guide you in the process of discerning God's guidance in planting a church in another culture, in order to fulfill his call in the Great Commission. Our prayer is that by the time you complete the exercises in this book you will come to understand the truths of Gospel ministry in such a way that you will be *spiritually and tactically ready* to plant a church. As a result, each session opens with worship and a devotional and ends in an extended prayer time, which are both essential aspects of your preparation to plant a church.

The five sessions represent the span of a church plant team's effort and ministry in a neighborhood or among a people group, from your initial prayer gathering to the time of transitioning the new church with its pastoral leaders. Each session is specifically designed to help you develop a portion of your church-planting strategic plan. The final session will help you wrap up the details in order to have a plan that you can execute under the guidance of the Holy Spirit.

The Guidebook's Structure: Understanding the Session Format

This book assumes that the teams that the Lord calls will possess different visions for the church, and will approach their church planting in various ways. Whether you are planting a church in your own culture, or planting a church cross-culturally, you will need to chart your own unique journey, being informed by the principles presented in this book. Whether planting a church in your own culture (i.e., intra cultural mission), or facing the complexities related to cross-cultural mission, we have provided additional notes and/or questions that will prompt you to consider issues relevant to your unique church plant opportunity. We will identify these notes and insights in their own section entitled "Charting Your Own Course." These sections are written to prompt you to consider how the material relates to your particular vision and work. Spend good time reflecting on the issues and questions covered in this section in order to get maximum benefit from the material in each session.

Source:
Ripe for Harvest,
pp. 11-22

Each of the five sessions follows this pattern:

- *Worship and Devotional*: some devotionals are available online (*www.tumi.org/churchplanting*) or you can teach your own devotional.

- *Session Themes and Objectives* will provide you with a general framework for both understanding and benefitting from the elements in each session. This section includes a listing of the main concept and objectives of each session, along with a key Scripture, a principle of spiritual warfare, the key principle of church planting, and a selected quote that helps illumine the session and its goals.

- *Seminar Teaching* on the important ideas you will need to consider before discussing your plan of action. Some of these seminars will be available as audio or video recordings at *www.tumi.org/churchplanting*. Many of the seminars are supported by helpful Appendices that should be carefully reviewed as part of the planning process. Each seminar concludes with a list of questions for group discussion.

- *Team Exercises* include a list of guiding questions to help you translate your discussion into concrete goals and action steps. The exercises are designed to be done together as a church-plant team, not individually or in isolation. Questions apply to the whole team unless otherwise noted. If you have not yet formed a core team (at least 2 others but no more than 10), make sure you do so before you start Session Two (Session One may be helpful in defining your vision so you can recruit a core team to join you).

There are eight team exercises in the book, and each exercise includes five parts:

- Guidelines

- Instructions

- Discussion Questions, Reading Assignments, or Worksheets

- Prayer

- Team Presentation

Source:
Ripe for Harvest,
pp. 11-22

The eight exercises build progressively on each other and are arranged around the PLANT acronym (see the table "Overview of Exercise Phases for World Impact's Evangel School of Urban Church Planting" in sessions 2-5). The table below lists the eight exercises in the order they appear.

Session	Team Exercise
Session 1, Team Exercise #1	Seeing the Big Picture: Establishing the Context
Session 1, Team Exercise #2	Seeing the Big Picture: Defining Values/Vision
Session 2, Team Exercise #3	Prepare: Be the Church
Session 3, Team Exercise #4	Launch: Expand the Church
Session 3, Team Exercise #5	Assemble: Establish the Church
Session 4, Team Exercise #6	Nurture: Mature the Church
Session 4, Team Exercise #7	Transition: Release the Church
Session 5, Team Exercise #8	Bringing It All Together: The Team Charter

- *Presentations*. One of the most helpful activities for your team will be sharing with other teams the results of your reflection and dialogue together. Each Session allows for you to share with others some of your more important insights, questions, and issues that you gleaned together from your Team Exercise discussion. Be open and observant during this activity – without a doubt, some of the best ideas you will hear will not necessarily be ones which you thought up! Allow the Lord to give you new ideas through the other team participants.

- *Charting Your Own Course*. Whether you are planting a church within your own culture, or within an association or denomination and you know what your make-up, governance, transition, and framework will be after the church is planted, this section is especially written for you. Here you will find specific notes of action steps or key principles that you should be aware of as you make plans to start the process of planting a church within your own culture or community. This section will ask you to bring

Source:
Ripe for Harvest,
pp. 11-22

your own, unique questions and context to bear on the material, for maximum benefit.

- *Further Resources*: Here you will find additional tools and helpful resources (e.g., bibliographies, suggested materials) that can be of use to you over the life of your church plant.

- *Appendices*: At the end of each session, you will see a listing of some key articles, graphics, and/or diagrams that are specifically related to the concepts in that lesson. All appendices can be found in the complimentary volumes connected with this guidebook entitled *Planting Churches among the City's Poor: An Anthology of Urban Church Planting Resources, Volumes I and II*. Please note: **These reference books are essential in order to receive maximum benefit from this guidebook. They should be purchased and used as a set.**

This is why these books are offered with this guidebook in the TUMI store [*www.tumistore.org*] at a discount, although each book can also be purchased individually. Please ensure that you have copies of the anthology handy for the various seminars, exercises, and discussions that make up each session's work.

The appendices are arranged at the end of each session, helping to both clarify and illumine the concepts and themes covered in the material. *Do not be alarmed if you see the same appendices referenced in different sessions.* This was done on purpose! If certain concepts need to be reiterated, underscored, or reemphasized, they may appear multiple times throughout the manual. Certain concepts are so fundamental that they will demand multiple looks, dialogues, and considerations. Do your best to think through the materials for the sake of bringing the key lessons of each session into greater focus, i.e., those tough concepts that you and your teammates will need to master along your church planting journey.

Coaching and Training with *Ripe for Harvest*

This book is designed to be best used in conjunction with the *Evangel Church Plant School*. Several issues should be highlighted regarding the materials both in *Ripe for Harvest* and its complimentary text, *Planting Churches among the City's Poor*.

The first issue is about **designations and terms**. Since *Planting Churches among the City's Poor* is essentially an anthology, we sought to preserve our earlier documents in their original form, and did not go back through the documents and revise the language used in our earliest schools. This is not a major difficulty, however, because although we use different

Source:
Ripe for Harvest,
pp. 11-22

terms than our earlier schools, we have maintained the same functions for the positions. Two terms need to be defined:

- In previous materials, the term used for the church planting supervisor or mentor to whom the team leader reported or received input from was called a **Multiple Team Leader** or **MTL**. Now, in this volume and in our schools, we refer to this role as **Coach**. All references to **MTL** or **Multiple Team Leader** in this volume or in *Planting Churches among the City's Poor* should be understood now as **Coach**.

- Also, in past schools we used the term **Team Leader** for the person in charge of the church plant team and church plant effort. Now, we refer to the person fulfilling this role as the **Church Planter**.

In terms of language, then, please remember that when you engage materials in the *Anthology* that cite *MTL* or *Multiple Team Leader*, they now ought to be understood as equivalent terms to *Coach*, and, the designation *Team Leader* is equivalent now to the designation *Church Planter*.

The second issue relates to **the various uses and applications** of *Ripe for Harvest* in the context of training and coaching church planters. *Evangel Schools* are offered around the world in conjunction with denominations, organizations, churches, and/or satellites of The Urban Ministry Institute (TUMI). For a list of currently scheduled schools, please go to *www.tumi.org/churchplanting*. Coaches, mentors, and planters can use *Ripe for Harvest* for church plant training in several ways.

To begin with, the normal mode of this guidebook's use will be a planter and his/her team attending a locally sponsored Evangel School training session. The exercises are designed for planters and their teams to reflect on the devotionals, seminar teaching, and then answer the questions in open dialogue. This is done to give them opportunity to clarify their own unique strategies and approaches as they plan out their engagement in a community or a people group, to plant a church.

Besides attending an *Evangel School*, a group of new church planters may decide to work through this book under the guidance of a church plant coach. Those using *Ripe for Harvest* in this way would be an example of a "Church Plant Cohort." The cohort may be sponsored by a denomination, a church planting group, or an Urban Church Association (UCA).

Source:
Ripe for Harvest,
pp. 11-22

A third way the book might be used is in a "one-on-one" context. A church planter and a church plant coach may decide to work through this book together doing the exercises in a one-on-one format. The one-on-one format still assumes that the church planter has a core team that participates in the process, but it allows the church planter and church plant coach to work through the team exercises and the PLANT process on a timeline that works best for their individual team.

Ultimately, it is the church planter who is responsible for leading the church plant team through the guidebook exercises. Yet our work with hundreds of urban church plants has convinced us that every Timothy needs a Paul. We encourage you to invite a trusted person to serve as a *Coach* throughout your planning process. A Coach can provide you with ongoing encouragement and challenge, giving you objective advice, assisting you when you get stuck, and holding you answerable for your target dates, as God leads.

Even if using this book in the one-on-one format, we suggest that you as a church planter and/or church plant team prepare presentations periodically for your coach to review and comment upon. You naturally could prepare such an overview presentation for each stage of your church planting, providing a clear snapshot of your planning for the upcoming phase. Presentations are a good way to ensure you are making your plans concrete enough to be executed.

Listed below is a representative sample of the kinds of questions that a Coach might consider in his/her coaching activities and process with a church planter and his/her team:

- How are the team members doing in their relationship with God? Are they regularly practicing their core spiritual disciplines?
- How are the team members' relationships with each other?
- How is their communication? Do they listen to each other? Is everyone being heard?
- Is there sufficient consensus within the team?
- Are they able to resolve issues as they come up?
- Do they understand the PWR (prepare/work/review) process? Are they showing indication that they will be able to flex and adjust their plan at a later time?
- Have they considered all the relevant points?
- Will they be able to implement their plans?

Source:
Ripe for Harvest,
pp. 11-22

- Are they teachable and open to the Lord, to the leader, and to one another?

- Did they understand the exercises and complete them satisfactorily?

- Is there strong leadership?

- Is the team and its members weighing their decisions in light of the Holy Spirit's leading and the principles of Scripture?

Obtaining Our "Church Planter's Tool Kit"

In addition to the guidebook and the anthology texts, we have put together a resource "kit" for church planters and their teams that provides a broad range of essential tools every church planter or team should possess as they prepare and begin their work to plant a church in the community God has called them to. If at all possible, obtain the tool-kit and familiarize yourself with these materials *before* you engage in the sessions included in this guidebook.

(Note: In the TUMI Store [*www.tumistore.org*], we have priced this kit affordably [the kit contains one each of the following] so you can obtain them all together, at a discount!)

- *Ripe for Harvest.* The fundamental resource guidebook for the Evangel School of Urban Church Planting

- *Planting Churches among the City's Poor: An Anthology of Urban Church Planting Resources, Volumes I and II.* A thorough and essential listing of World Impact's historical papers, diagrams, and insights into the issues and opportunities associated with urban cross-cultural church planting among the urban poor.

- *Jesus Cropped from the Picture: Why Christians Get Bored and How to Restore them to Vibrant Faith.* An insightful analysis of the reasons behind the demise of the American evangelical church, and how to fix it.

- *Sacred Roots: A Primer on Retrieving the Great Tradition.* A sequel to *Jesus Cropped from the Picture,* this is an informative introduction to the power of shared spirituality of the ancient church, and how a return to those roots can transform the contemporary church.

- *Fight the Good Fight of Faith.* A clear, concise, and biblical introduction to the first truths of the Christian faith (and TUMI's official pre-Capstone curriculum). It is designed especially for new Christians and helps them understand what the Bible says

Source:
Ripe for Harvest,
pp. 11-22

about participating in God's grand story through nine integrated lessons from the book of Ephesians.

- *The Heroic Venture: A Parable of Project Leadership.* A manual on how to plan, implement, and lead important ministry projects, using lessons gleaned from the Lewis and Clark expedition to help us chart the way.

- *Managing Projects for Ministry.* A TUMI Course textbook, this practical how-to manual lays out the specific activities in designing, implementing, controlling, and wrapping up effective ministry projects – done on time, within budget, and according to specifications.

- *TUMI Sacred Roots Annual.* A yearly thematic devotional guide that employs the Christian year and an annual theme to aid disciples to walk in shared spirituality as a body together.

- *The Church Year Calendar.* A tool based on the Christian year to help believers walk together throughout the year focused on the life and ministry of Christ.

- *The SIAFU Network Guidebook*: A one-step guidebook on how to mobilize men and women in the local church for mission to their community and ministry to one another.

- *The SIAFU Network Chapter Meeting Guide*: A practical guide to show you how to set up and conduct your SIAFU Chapter gatherings so that your members will feel welcomed, refreshed, and encouraged as they worship, testify, and challenge each other in Christ.

- *Let God Arise!* The longer title of this book explains a bit more about its content: *Let God Arise: A Sober Call to Prevailing Prayer for a Dynamic Spiritual Awakening and the Aggressive Advancement of th Kingdom in America's Inner Cities.* This short booklet lays out a rationale for why every local urban church needs to be deeply committed to prayer.

In addition to the excellent resources in this kit, we also recommend the following tools that provide helpful insight in your outreach to the community, discipling the faithful, and empowering emerging leaders as God raises them up:

- *Making Joyful Noises: Mastering the Fundamentals of Music.* A primer on music theory and leading effective worship leading.

- *Vision for Mission: Nurturing an Apostolic Heart.* This eight-session study course describes the heart of a church planter viewed through the lens of the men who "turned the world

Source:
Ripe for Harvest,
pp. 11-22

upside down" It is part of TUMI's Foundations for Ministry Series and available through local TUMI satellites or online at *www.tumistore.org.*

- *Focus on Reproduction, Module 12, The Capstone Curriculum.* This eight-session study on urban church planting is module 12 of 16 in TUMI's *Capstone Curriculum.* The other three modules in the urban mission track of the *Capstone Curriculum* also provide vital resources for urban church planters (e.g. training on spiritual warfare, evangelism, mission to the poor, theology of the city, mercy ministries, etc.) and are available through local TUMI satellites or online at *www.tumistore.org.*

- *Winning the World: Facilitating Urban Church Planting Movements.* This eight-session study on Church Plant Movements is part of TUMI's *Foundations for Ministry Series.* It provides an important big picture overview of what the Holy Spirit is doing around the world through Church Plant Movements. It encourages church planters and church plant coaches to make a paradigm shift from focusing on single church plants to movements of church plants. This course is available through local TUMI satellites and at both www.tumistore.org and at *www.biblicaltraining.org.*

- *Church Matters: Retrieving the Great Tradition.* This eight-session study is part of TUMI's *Foundations for Ministry Series.* It provides an overview of the history of the Church and its Great Tradition which is essential context for any church planters unfamiliar with the Church's "Family History." This course is available through local TUMI satellites and at *www.tumistore.org.*

- *Marking Time: Forming Spirituality through the Christian Year.* This eight-session study is part of TUMI's *Foundations for Ministry Series.* It provides a strategy for discipleship and shared spirituality in the church using the Christian year. For church planters who have never considered their theology of time, this course is absolutely essential. It introduces a simple and reproducible system for discipleship, preaching, and spiritual formation gleaned from the example of the early church – a church primarily made up of the urban poor. This course is available through local TUMI satellites and at *www.tumistore.org.*

- *Multiplying Laborers for the Urban Harvest: Shifting the Paradigm for Servant Leadership Education.* Each church planter must figure out how to develop new leaders and The Urban Ministry Institute (TUMI) was founded in 1995 to help church planters with this task. Multiplying Laborers is a book that lays out a system for how each local church or network of local churches can provide excellent theological training for leaders in their

Source:
Ripe for Harvest,
pp. 11-22

own ministry context. In 2015, over two hundred urban churches and urban ministries have launched satellite campuses for training their leaders. This book is available at *www.tumistore.org.*

Supplies for the Journey: *www.tumi.org*

Among other things, The Urban Ministry Institute designs and produces resources for urban mission, specifically for the planting and multiplication of churches, and the empowerment of church movements, especially among the poor. For instance, in addition to the booklet, *Let God Arise!*, you will find on our site a plethora of resources to help you lay the groundwork of your church plant in prayer through the larger collection of *Let God Arise! Prayer Resources.* There are a constellation of resources available for evangelism, equipping, and empowering (see especially the *Master the Bible System*, and the *SIAFU* Resources).

Perhaps the most significant resource available to your new church plant is the sixteen module Capstone Curriculum. The sixteen modules provide seminary quality training for your church plant team members and emerging leaders. One church in the Los Angeles area has trained over one hundred leaders and planted twenty churches in five countries using the Capstone Curriculum as their primary leadership development tool. If your church plant is interested in launching your own training center you may want to consider launching a TUMI satellite at your church at some point in the PLANT process. In short, be sure to browse our site and become familiar with the many helpful resources for church planting and church life at *www.tumi.org/churchplanting.*

We have recorded the videos for each Session Seminar, which are available for either viewing or download at the following web page *www.tumi.org/churchplanting.* Our intent is to make these church planting materials available to the broadest possible audience, providing individuals, denominations, local churches, Urban Church Associations (UCAs), organizations, and missions groups with quality, clear materials that can equip a new generation of church planters who can raise up outposts in the most dangerous and least empowered communities in America and around the world. We assume your interest in this guide-book and anthology reveals your sharing this passion, this church planting DNA and vision.

A Vision for Our Time

Please know, our singular end is to find ways to outfit, encourage, and resource as many as we can with the kind of training and tools that make church planting among the poor a constant and effective ministry for years to come. We are ever open to your comments and suggestions,

Source:
Ripe for Harvest,
pp. 11-22

so please, do not hesitate to contact us – if you want to partner or link arms with us as we strive to raise up outposts of the Kingdom in the neediest communities on earth.

Immediately following his encounter with the Samaritan woman, she ran into the town and said to the people that she had found a man who had told her all that she had ever done. Surely, she said, this must be the Christ! Meanwhile, the disciples returned from their errand to get food, and urged him to eat. Jesus told them that his food was to do God's will and to finish his work. Then he replied, "Do you not say, 'There are yet four months, then comes the harvest'? Look, I tell you, lift up your eyes, and see that the fields are white [ripe] for harvest (John 4.35 ESV). The name for this guidebook is derived from this statement of our Lord. We have lifted up our eyes on the unreached urban poor, and know them to be fields fully mature, ripe for harvest. It is in the spirit of this readiness that we write this volume, penned for those who see the ripened fields and are ready to plant healthy churches among the poor in the cities of the world.

Remember what our Lord said of the dying millions, a word that still fits the urban poor today:

> Matthew 9.35-38 (ESV) – And Jesus went throughout all the cities and villages, teaching in their synagogues and proclaiming the gospel of the kingdom and healing every disease and every affliction. When he saw the crowds, he had compassion for them, because they were harassed and helpless, like sheep without a shepherd. Then he said to his disciples, "The harvest is plentiful, but the laborers are few; therefore pray earnestly to the Lord of the harvest to send out laborers into his harvest."

May the Lord send out laborers into his harvest, among the urban poor peoples of this world, and may his Kingdom advance among them, to the glory of God. We are convinced that God will surprise us all as he works on their behalf, in places which have yet to experience his saving grace and love.

Rev. Don Allsman
Los Angeles, CA

Rev. Dr. Hank Voss
Los Angeles, CA

Rev. Dr. Don L. Davis
Wichita, KS

Introduction
Sacred Roots, Church Planting, and the Great Tradition

Source:
Ripe for Harvest,
pp. 23-28

Sacred Roots, Church Planting, and the Great Tradition

This essay was previously entitled "Going Forward by Looking Back: Toward an Evangelical Retrieval of the Great Tradition" by Don L. Davis (Wichita: TUMI Press, 2008). We are inserting it here as a fine introduction to this guidebook, since it concisely explains the fundamental importance of rediscovering the roots of our faith in our theology, worship, discipleship, and mission. We are convinced that we must place our activity of evangelism, discipleship, church planting, and mission in the context of what the Church has done and believed – always, everywhere, and by all of us. As church planters we must rediscover the apostolic faith, contextualize it among particular people groups, and then train them to express culturally that faith in a way that defends, extends, and embodies the one, true faith which the Church has always held. For those of us who long to see the Good News come alive in places where Jesus has never been known (i.e., the world's urban poor), this message is essential for us to remember – and to relearn. As we progress through the stages of church planting among the city's poor, we must stay aware of these insights, and strive to implement them in every facet of our outreach and empowerment.

Rediscovering the "Great Tradition"

In a wonderful little book, Ola Tjorhom,[1] describes the Great Tradition of the Church (sometimes called the "classical Christian tradition") as "living, organic, and dynamic."[2] The Great Tradition represents that evangelical, apostolic, and catholic core of Christian faith and practice which came largely to fruition from 100-500 AD.[3] Its rich legacy and treasures represent the Church's confession of what the Church has always believed, the worship that the ancient, undivided Church celebrated and embodied, and the mission that it embraced and undertook.

While the Great Tradition can neither substitute for the Apostolic Tradition (i.e., the authoritative source of all Christian faith, the Scriptures), nor should it overshadow the living presence of Christ in the Church through the Holy Spirit, it is still authoritative and revitalizing for the people of God. It has and still can provide God's people through time with the substance of its confession and faith. The Great Tradition has been embraced and affirmed as authoritative by Catholic, Orthodox, Anglican, and Protestant theologians, those ancient and modern, as it has produced the seminal documents, doctrines, confessions, and practices of the Church (e.g., the canon of Scriptures, the doctrines of the Trinity, the deity of Christ, etc.).

Source:
Ripe for Harvest,
pp. 23-28

Many evangelical scholars today believe that the way forward for dynamic faith and spiritual renewal will entail looking back, not with sentimental longings for the "good old days" of a pristine, problem free early Church, or a naive and even futile attempt to ape their heroic journey of faith. Rather, with a critical eye to history, a devout spirit of respect for the ancient Church, and a deep commitment to Scripture, we ought to rediscover through the Great Tradition the seeds of a new, authentic, and empowered faith. We can be transformed as we retrieve and are informed by the core beliefs and practices of the Church before the horrible divisions and fragmentations of Church history.

Well, if we do believe we ought to at least look again at the early Church and its life, or better yet, are convinced even to retrieve the Great Tradition for the sake of renewal in the Church–what exactly are we hoping to get back? Are we to uncritically accept everything the ancient Church said and did as "gospel," to be truthful simply because it is closer to the amazing events of Jesus of Nazareth in the world? Is old "hip," in and of itself?

No. We neither accept all things uncritically, nor do we believe that old, in and of itself, is truly good. Truth for us is more than ideas or ancient claims; for us, truth was incarnated in the person of Jesus of Nazareth, and the Scriptures give authoritative and final claim to the meaning of his revelation and salvation in history. We cannot accept things simply because they are reported to have been done in the past, or begun in the past. Amazingly, the Great Tradition itself argued for us to be critical, to contend for the faith once delivered to the saints (Jude 3), to embrace and celebrate the tradition received from the Apostles, rooted and interpreted by the Holy Scriptures themselves, and expressed in Christian confession and practice.

Core Dimensions of the Great Tradition
While Tjorhom offers his own list of ten elements of the theological content of the Great Tradition that he believes is worthy of reinterpretation and regard,[4] I believe there are seven dimensions that, from a biblical and spiritual vantage point, can enable us to understand what the early Church believed, how they worshiped and lived, and the ways they defended their living faith in Jesus Christ. Through their allegiance to the documents, confessions, and practices of this period, the ancient Church bore witness to God's salvation promise in the midst of a pagan and crooked generation. The core of our current faith and practice was developed in this era, and deserves a second (and twenty-second) look.

Adapting, redacting, and extending Tjorhom's notions of the Great Tradition, I list here what I take to be, as a start, a simple listing of the

Source:
Ripe for Harvest,
pp. 23-28

critical dimensions that deserve our undivided attention and wholehearted retrieval.

The Apostolic Tradition. The Great Tradition is rooted in the Apostolic Tradition, i.e., the apostles' eyewitness testimony and firsthand experience of Jesus of Nazareth, their authoritative witness to his life and work recounted in the Holy Scriptures, the canon of our Bible today. The Church is apostolic, built on the foundation of the prophets and the apostles, with Christ himself being the Cornerstone. The Scriptures themselves represent the source of our interpretation about the Kingdom of God, that story of God's redemptive love embodied in the promise to Abraham and the patriarchs, in the covenants and experience of Israel, and which culminates in the revelation of God in Christ Jesus, as predicted in the prophets and explicated in the apostolic testimony.

The Ecumenical Councils and Creeds, Especially the Nicene Creed. The Great Tradition declares the truth and sets the bounds of the historic orthodox faith as defined and asserted in the ecumenical creeds of the ancient and undivided Church, with special focus on the Nicene Creed. Their declarations were taken to be an accurate interpretation and commentary on the teachings of the Apostles set in Scripture. While not the source of the Faith itself, the confession of the ecumenical councils and creeds represents the substance of its teachings,[5] especially those before the fifth century (where virtually all of the elemental doctrines concerning God, Christ, and salvation were articulated and embraced).[6]

The Ancient Rule of Faith. The Great Tradition embraced the substance of this core Christian faith in a rule, i.e., an ancient standard rule of faith, that was considered to be the yardstick by which claims and propositions regarding the interpretation of the biblical faith were to be assessed. This rule, when applied reverently and rigorously, can clearly allow us to define the core Christian confession of the ancient and undivided Church expressed clearly in that instruction and adage of Vincent of Lerins: "that which has always been believed, everywhere, and by all."[7]

The *Christus Victor* Worldview. The Great Tradition celebrates and affirms Jesus of Nazareth as the Christ, the promised Messiah of the Hebrew Scriptures, the risen and exalted Lord, and Head of the Church. In Jesus of Nazareth alone, God has reasserted his reign over the universe, having destroyed death in his dying, conquering God's enemies through his incarnation, death, resurrection, and ascension, and ransoming humanity from its penalty due to its transgression of the Law. Now resurrected from the dead, ascended and exalted at the right hand of God, he has sent the Holy Spirit into the world to empower the Church in its life and witness. The Church is to be considered the

Source:
Ripe for Harvest,
pp. 23-28

people of the victory of Christ. At his return, he will consummate his work as Lord. This worldview was expressed in the ancient Church's confession, preaching, worship, and witness. Today, through its liturgy and practice of the Church Year, the Church acknowledges, celebrates, embodies, and proclaims this victory of Christ: the destruction of sin and evil and the restoration of all creation.

The Centrality of the Church. The Great Tradition confidently confessed the Church as the people of God. The faithful assembly of believers, under the authority of the Shepherd Christ Jesus, is now the locus and agent of the Kingdom of God on earth. In its worship, fellowship, teaching, service, and witness, Christ continues to live and move. The Great Tradition insists that the Church, under the authority of its undershepherds and the entirety of the priesthood of believers, is visibly the dwelling of God in the Spirit in the world today. With Christ himself being the Chief Cornerstone, the Church is the family of God, the body of Christ, and the temple of the Holy Spirit. All believers, living, dead, and yet unborn – make up the one, holy, catholic (universal), and apostolic community. Gathering together regularly in believing assembly, members of the Church meet locally to worship God through Word and sacrament, and to bear witness in its good works and pro-clamation of the Gospel. Incorporating new believers into the Church through baptism, the Church embodies the life of the Kingdom in its fellowship, and demonstrates in word and deed the reality of the Kingdom of God through its life together and service to the world.

The Unity of the Faith. The Great Tradition affirms unequivocally the catholicity of the Church of Jesus Christ, in that it is concerned with keeping communion and continuity with the worship and theology of the Church throughout the ages (Church universal). Since there has been and can only be one hope, calling, and faith, the Great Tradition fought and strove for oneness in word, in doctrine, in worship, in charity.

The Evangelical Mandate of the Risen Christ. The Great Tradition affirms the apostolic mandate to make known to the nations the victory of God in Jesus Christ, proclaiming salvation by grace through faith in his name, and inviting all peoples to repentance and faith to enter into the Kingdom of God. Through acts of justice and righteousness, the Church displays the life of the Kingdom in the world today, and through its preaching and life together provides a witness and sign of the Kingdom present in and for the world (*sacramentum mundi*), and as the pillar and ground of the truth. As evidence of the Kingdom of God and custodians of the Word of God, the Church is charged to define clearly and defend the faith once for all delivered to the Church by the apostles.

Source:
Ripe for Harvest,
pp. 23-28

Conclusion: Finding Our Future by Looking Back

In a time where so many are confused by the noisy chaos of so many claiming to speak for God, it is high time for us to rediscover the roots of our faith, to go back to the beginning of Christian confession and practice, and see, if in fact, we can recover our identity in the stream of Christ worship and discipleship that changed the world. In my judgment, this can be done through a critical, evangelical appropriation of the Great Tradition, that core belief and practice which is the source of all our traditions, whether Catholic, Orthodox, Anglican, or Protestant.

Of course, specific traditions will continue to seek to express and live out their commitment to the Authoritative Tradition (i.e., the Scriptures) and Great Tradition through their worship, teaching, and service. Our diverse Christian traditions (little "t"), when they are rooted in and expressive of the teaching of Scripture and led by the Holy Spirit, will continue to make the Gospel clear within new cultures or sub-cultures, speaking and modeling the hope of Christ into new situations shaped by their own set of questions posed in light of their own unique circumstances. Our traditions are essentially movements of contextualization, that is, they are attempts to make plain within people groups the Authoritative Tradition in a way that faithfully and effectively leads them to faith in Jesus Christ.

We ought, therefore, to find ways to enrich our contemporary traditions by reconnecting and integrating our contemporary confessions and practices with the Great Tradition. Let us never forget that Christianity, at its core, is a faithful witness to God's saving acts in history. As such, we will always be a people who seek to find our futures by looking back through time at those moments of revelation and action where the Rule of God was made plain through the incarnation, passion, resurrection, ascension, and soon-coming of Christ. Let us then remember, celebrate, reenact, learn afresh, and passionately proclaim what believers have confessed since the morning of the empty tomb–the saving story of God's promise in Jesus of Nazareth to redeem and save a people for his own.

Endnotes

1   Ola Tjorhom, *Visible Church–Visible Unity: Ecumenical Ecclesiology and "The Great Tradition of the Church."* Collegeville, Minnesota: Liturgical Press, 2004. Robert Webber defined the Great Tradition in this way: "[It is] the broad outline of Christian belief and practice developed from the Scriptures between the time of Christ and the middle of the fifth century." Robert E. Webber, *The Majestic Tapestry.* Nashville: Thomas Nelson Publishers, 1986, p. 10.

2   Ibid., p. 35.

Source:
Ripe for Harvest,
pp. 23-28

3   The core of the Great Tradition concentrates on the formulations, confessions, and practices of the Church's first five centuries of life and work. Thomas Oden, in my judgment, rightly asserts that ". . . . most of what is enduringly valuable in contemporary biblical exegesis was discovered by the fifth century" (cf. Thomas C. Oden, *The Word of Life.* San Francisco: HarperSanFrancisco, 1989, p. xi.).

4   Ibid., pp. 27-29. Tjorhom's ten elements are argued in the context of his work where he also argues for the structural elements and the ecumenical implications of retrieving the Great Tradition. I wholeheartedly agree with the general thrust of his argument, which, like my own belief, makes the claim that an interest in and study of the Great Tradition can renew and enrich the contemporary Church in its worship, service, and mission.

5   I am indebted to the late Dr. Robert E. Webber for this helpful distinction between the source and the substance of Christian faith and interpretation.

6   While the seven ecumenical Councils (along with others) are affirmed by both Catholic and Orthodox communions as binding, it is the first four Councils that are to be considered the critical, most essential confessions of the ancient, undivided Church. I and others argue for this largely because the first four articulate and settle once and for all what is to be considered our orthodox faith on the doctrines of the Trinity and the Incarnation (cf. Philip Schaff, *The Creeds of Christendom*, v. 1. Grand Rapids: Baker Book House, 1996, p. 44). Similarly, even the magisterial Reformers embraced the teaching of the Great Tradition, and held its most significant confessions as authoritative. Correspondingly, Calvin could argue in his own theological interpretations that "Thus councils would come to have the majesty that is their due; yet in the meantime Scripture would stand out in the higher place, with everything subject to its standard. In this way, we willingly embrace and reverence as holy the early councils, such as those of Nicea, Constantinople, the first of Ephesus I, Chalcedon, and the like, which were concerned with refuting errors – in so far as they relate to the teachings of faith. For they contain nothing but the pure and genuine exposition of Scripture, which the holy Fathers applied with spiritual prudence to crush the enemies of religion who had then arisen" (cf. John Calvin, *Institutes of the Christian Religion*, IV, ix. 8. John T. McNeill, ed. Ford Lewis Battles, trans. Philadelphia: Westminster Press, 1960, pp. 1171-72).

7   This rule, which has won well-deserved favor down through the years as a sound theological yardstick for authentic Christian truth, weaves three cords of critical assessment to determine what may be counted as orthodox or not in the Church's teaching. St. Vincent of Lerins, a theological commentator who died before 450 AD, authored what has come to be called the "Vincentian canon, a three-fold test of catholicity: *quod ubique, quod semper, quod ab omnibus creditum est* (what has been believed everywhere, always and by all). By this three-fold test of ecumenicity, antiquity, and consent, the church may discern between true and false traditions." (cf. Thomas C. Oden, *Classical Pastoral Care*, vol. 4. Grand Rapids: Baker Books, 1987, p. 243).

A Call to an Ancient Evangelical Future

Robert Webber and Phil Kenyon • Revised 36 - 5.12.06 Prologue

Source:
Ripe for Harvest,
pp. 83-86

Prologue

In every age the Holy Spirit calls the Church to examine its faithfulness to God's revelation in Jesus Christ, authoritatively recorded in Scripture and handed down through the Church. Thus, while we affirm the global strength and vitality of worldwide Evangelicalism in our day, we believe the North American expression of Evangelicalism needs to be especially sensitive to the new external and internal challenges facing God's people.

These external challenges include the current cultural milieu and the resurgence of religious and political ideologies. The internal challenges include Evangelical accommodation to civil religion, rationalism, privatism and pragmatism. In light of these challenges, we call Evangelicals to strengthen their witness through a recovery of the faith articulated by the consensus of the ancient Church and its guardians in the traditions of Eastern Orthodoxy, Roman Catholicism, the Protestant Reformation and the Evangelical awakenings. Ancient Christians faced a world of paganism, Gnosticism and political domination. In the face of heresy and persecution, they understood history through Israel's story, culminating in the death and resurrection of Jesus and the coming of God's Kingdom.

Today, as in the ancient era, the Church is confronted by a host of master narratives that contradict and compete with the gospel. The pressing question is: who gets to narrate the world? The Call to an Ancient Evangelical Future challenges Evangelical Christians to restore the priority of the divinely inspired biblical story of God's acts in history. The narrative of God's Kingdom holds eternal implications for the mission of the Church, its theological reflection, its public ministries of worship and spirituality and its life in the world. By engaging these themes, we believe the Church will be strengthened to address the issues of our day.

1. On the Primacy of the Biblical Narrative

We call for a return to the priority of the divinely authorized canonical story of the Triune God. This story – Creation, Incarnation, and Re-creation – was effected by Christ's recapitulation of human history and summarized by the early Church in its Rules of Faith. The gospel-formed content of these Rules served as the key to the interpretation of Scripture and its critique of contemporary culture, and thus shaped the church's pastoral ministry. Today, we call Evangelicals to turn away from modern theological methods that reduce the gospel to mere propositions, and

Context
Values/Vision
Prepare
Launch
Assemble
Nurture
Transition
Schedule/Charter

Source:
Ripe for Harvest,
pp. 83-86

from contemporary pastoral ministries so compatible with culture that they camouflage God's story or empty it of its cosmic and redemptive meaning. In a world of competing stories, we call Evangelicals to recover the truth of God's word as the story of the world, and to make it the centerpiece of Evangelical life.

2. On the Church, the Continuation of God's Narrative

We call Evangelicals to take seriously the visible character of the Church. We call for a commitment to its mission in the world in fidelity to God's mission (*Missio Dei*), and for an exploration of the ecumenical implications this has for the unity, holiness catholicity, and apostolicity of the Church. Thus, we call Evangelicals to turn away from an individualism that makes the Church a mere addendum to God's redemptive plan. Individualistic Evangelicalism has contributed to the current problems of churchless Christianity, redefinitions of the Church according to business models, separatist ecclesiologies and judgmental attitudes toward the Church. Therefore, we call Evangelicals to recover their place in the community of the Church catholic.

3. On the Church's Theological Reflection on God's Narrative

We call for the Church's reflection to remain anchored in the Scriptures in continuity with the theological interpretation learned from the early Fathers. Thus, we call Evangelicals to turn away from methods that separate theological reflection from the common traditions of the Church. These modern methods compartmentalize God's story by analyzing its separate parts, while ignoring God's entire redemptive work as recapitulated in Christ. Anti-historical attitudes also disregard the common biblical and theological legacy of the ancient Church. Such disregard ignores the hermeneutical value of the Church's ecumenical creeds. This reduces God's story of the world to one of many competing theologies and impairs the unified witness of the Church to God's plan for the history of the world. Therefore, we call Evangelicals to unity in "the tradition that has been believed everywhere, always and by all," as well as to humility and charity in their various Protestant traditions.

4. On Church's Worship as Telling and Enacting God's Narrative

We call for public worship that sings, preaches and enacts God's story. We call for a renewed consideration of how God ministers to us in baptism, eucharist, confession, the laying on of hands, marriage, healing and through the charisms of the Spirit, for these actions shape our lives and signify the meaning of the world. Thus, we call Evangelicals to turn away from forms of worship that focus on God as a mere object of the intellect, or that assert the self as the source of worship. Such worship has resulted in lecture-oriented, music-driven, performance-centered and program-controlled models that do not adequately proclaim God's

Context
Values/Vision
Prepare
Launch
Assemble
Nurture
Transition
Schedule/Charter

Source:
Ripe for Harvest,
pp. 83-86

cosmic redemption. Therefore, we call Evangelicals to recover the historic substance of worship of Word and Table and to attend to the Christian year, which marks time according to God's saving acts.

5. On Spiritual Formation in the Church as Embodiment of God's Narrative

We call for a catechetical spiritual formation of the people of God that is based firmly on a Trinitarian biblical narrative. We are concerned when spirituality is separated from the story of God and baptism into the life of Christ and his Body. Spirituality, made independent from God's story, is often characterized by legalism, mere intellectual knowledge, an overly therapeutic culture, New Age Gnosticism, a dualistic rejection of this world and a narcissistic preoccupation with one's own experience. These false spiritualities are inadequate for the challenges we face in today's world. Therefore, we call Evangelicals to return to a historic spirituality like that taught and practiced in the ancient catechumenate.

6. On the Church's Embodied Life in the World

We call for a cruciform holiness and commitment to God's mission in the world. This embodied holiness affirms life, biblical morality and appropriate self-denial. It calls us to be faithful stewards of the created order and bold prophets to our contemporary culture. Thus, we call Evangelicals to intensify their prophetic voice against forms of indifference to God's gift of life, economic and political injustice, ecological insensitivity and the failure to champion the poor and marginalized. Too often we have failed to stand prophetically against the culture's captivity to racism, consumerism, political correctness, civil religion, sexism, ethical relativism, violence and the culture of death. These failures have muted the voice of Christ to the world through his Church and detract from God's story of the world, which the Church is collectively to embody. Therefore, we call the Church to recover its counter-cultural mission to the world.

Epilogue

In sum, we call Evangelicals to recover the conviction that God's story shapes the mission of the Church to bear witness to God's Kingdom and to inform the spiritual foundations of civilization. We set forth this Call as an ongoing, open-ended conversation. We are aware that we have our blind spots and weaknesses. Therefore, we encourage Evangelicals to engage this Call within educational centers, denominations and local churches through publications and conferences.

We pray that we can move with intention to proclaim a loving, transcendent, triune God who has become involved in our history. In line with Scripture, creed and tradition, it is our deepest desire

Context
Values/Vision
Prepare
Launch
Assemble
Nurture
Transition
Schedule/Charter

Source:
Ripe for Harvest,
pp. 83-86

to embody God's purposes in the mission of the Church through our theological reflection, our worship, our spirituality and our life in the world, all the while proclaiming that Jesus is Lord over all creation.

© Northern Seminary 2006 Robert Webber and Phil Kenyon Permission is granted to reproduce the Call in unaltered form with proper citation.

Sponsors

Northern Seminary (*www.seminary.edu*)
Baker Books (*www.bakerbooks.com*)
Institute for Worship Studies (*www.iwsfla.org*)
InterVarsity Press (*www.ivpress.com*)

This Call is issued in the spirit of sic et non; therefore those who affix their names to this Call need not agree with all its content. Rather, its consensus is that these are issues to be discussed in the tradition of *semper reformanda* as the church faces the new challenges of our time. Over a period of seven months, more than 300 persons have participated via e-mail to write the Call. These men and women represent a broad diversity of ethnicity and denominational affiliation.

The four theologians who most consistently interacted with the development of the Call have been named as *Theological Editors*. The *Board of Reference* was given the special assignment of overall approval.

If you wish to be a signer on the *Call* go to *www.ancientfuturefaithnetwork.org.*

Context
Values/Vision
Prepare
Launch
Assemble
Nurture
Transition
Schedule/Charter

Church Planting Models

Rev. Dr. Don L. Davis

Source:
Ripe for Harvest,
pp. 87-89

The following models represent a spectrum of models which have been associated with evangelical church planting. Questions are designed to help us explore the various options available to the cross-cultural urban church planter in establishing congregations among the poor. Our dialogue today hopefully will isolate some of the critical issues necessary for a church plant team to think through in order to make its selection as to what particular kind of church they ought to plant, given the culture, population, and other factors encountered in its particular mission field.

1. What is the definition of the phrase "church planting models"? Why might it be important to consider various options in planting a church among the poor in the city?

2. How would you characterize the various models (or other) which have been allowed or employed in traditional church planting? What would you consider to be its strengths and/or weaknesses, and should we use any of them in our planting of churches among the poor in the city?

   a. Founding Pastor Model – a leader moves into a community with a commitment to lead and shepherd the church that is planted.

   b. Church Split Model?! – a new church is formed due to fundamental disagreement over some issue of morality, Bible interpretation, or schism.

   c. Nucleus Model – (sometimes referred to as the "colonization" model). This model involves a central assembly commissioning a smaller nucleus from its group (usually with leadership and members already organized) to leave the larger assembly and relocate into an unreached community as a kind of ready-made nucleus of the church which is to be formed.

   d. Beachhead or Mother Church Model – a strong, central congregation determines to become a kind of sending center and nurturing headquarters for new churches planted through its oversight and auspices, in the immediate area and/or beyond.

Context
Values/Vision
Prepare
Launch
Assemble
Nurture
Transition
Schedule/Charter

Source:
Ripe for Harvest,
pp. 87-89

e. Cell Church Model – once centralized assembly which considers the heart of its life and ministry to occur in the cells which are connected structurally and pastorally to the central congregation; their participation together constitutes the church.

f. Home Church Model – a church, which although similar to a cell church model, is intentionally planted with greater attention given to the authority and autonomy of the gathering of Christians who meet regularly in their respective homes.

g. Missionary Model – a church where a cross-cultural church planter seeks to plant a church among an unreached people with an intent from the beginning to help the church to be self-propagating, self-governing, and self-supporting.

3. Instead of models language, World Impact recognizes three distinct "expressions" of church planting, out of which various models can be considered and employed.

The Small Church Expression (or "house church," 20-50 people). The small (or house) church can be understood as a *small store in a shopping mall.* It needs the connections to other small churches to both survive and thrive. Small churches are able to meet virtually anywhere and can operate with a tiny footprint with little to no financial burdens. They can focus on a specific block, housing development, or network of families. This expression allows for a strong discipleship focus of indigenous leadership development which can take place in this smaller connected group.

The Community Church Expression (60-150 people)
The community church is the most common expression of church, numerically speaking, in the world today. This expression can be understood as a *grocery or convenience store in a neighborhood or community.* This expression focuses on a particular geographic identity and proximity, highlighting both the affinity, connection, and unique context of the congregation and the surrounding community. It is developed around a deep calling and connection to a particular neighborhood, and typically requires a semi-stable place to meet (e.g., a park, community center, or school). Partnership with other community churches is important.

The Mother Church Expression (200+ people)
The mother church (or "hub church") represents a larger assembly of believers, and can be understood as *a Walmart Superstore or Super*

Context
Values/Vision
Prepare
Launch
Assemble
Nurture
Transition
Schedule/Charter

Source:
Ripe for Harvest,
pp. 87-89

Target, a store which houses a number of select entities that supply its patrons with many choices and opportunities. This kind of church, which has both the economic and spiritual resources for multiplication, can leverage its resources and capabilities to become both a sending/empowering church which reproduces itself many times over. Ideally, a mother or hub church is a congregation that is led by clear missional intents that allow it to leverage its capabilities and gifts to become a center of compassion, mercy, and justice ministries. It can also come to serve as the nurturing headquarters for church planters and ministry starters, and can easily operate as an incubator of other effective ministries among the unreached urban poor. Such an expression usually is more rooted in a particular built-to-suit facility that allows it to leverage these kinds of capabilities.

4. What are the critical issues (e.g., culture, the tradition of the church planters, and contextualization) which ought to be factored most into selecting the appropriate model or expression for use in planting a church cross-culturally in the city?

5. Of all the things which a church planter may be aware of, what do you believe is the central element he or she must understand in order to choose the "right" option for them?

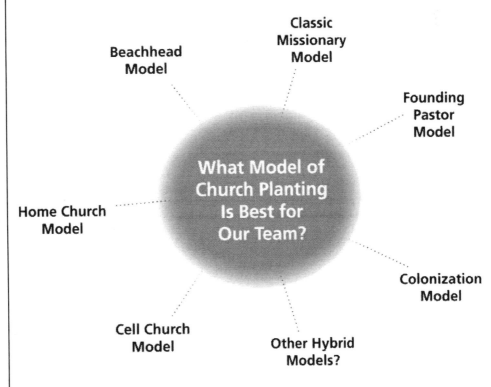

Context
Values/Vision
Prepare
Launch
Assemble
Nurture
Transition
Schedule/Charter

On World Impact's "Empowering the Urban Poor"

Rev. Dr. Don L. Davis

Source:
Ripe for Harvest,
pp. 195-200

Since our founding more than forty years ago, World Impact has spoken prophetically regarding God's election of the poor, the benign neglect of the evangelical church of America's inner city poor, and the need for evangelism, discipleship, and church planting in unreached urban poor communities. We believe that credible urban mission must demonstrate the Gospel, testifying in both the proclaimed word and concrete action. In light of this, we have emphasized living in the communities we serve, ministering to the needs of the whole person, as well as to the members of the whole urban family. We have sought this witness with a goal to see communities reached and transformed by Christ, believing that those who live in the city and are poor can be empowered to live in the freedom, wholeness, and justice of the Kingdom of God fleshed out in local churches and viable urban church planting movements. All our vision, prayer, and efforts are concentrated on a particular social group, the "urban poor," and our commitment to "empower" them through all facets of our work.

While the phrase "the urban poor" may be misunderstood or misused, we have chosen to employ it with our own stipulated meanings, informed by biblical theology as well as urban sociology. We employ the term to identify those whom God has commissioned us to serve, as well as to represent God's prophetic call to proclaim Good News to the poor, both to the church and to our society at large.

It must be conceded, of course, that the term "urban poor" may be easily misapplied and misused. The American city is dramatically diverse, profoundly complex in its mixtures of classes, cultures, and ethnicities. Amid so much diversity, a phrase like "the urban poor" may, at first glance, appear to be too denotative to be suitable as a summary designation of those whom we serve, being somewhat dry and academic. Without clearly stipulating what you mean when you use it, it can easily turn to mere labeling, which tends to reinforce stereotypes, encouraging generalizations about city dwellers which are either too vague or generic to be useful.

Context
Values/Vision
Prepare
Launch
Assemble
Nurture
Transition
Schedule/Charter

Further, some might even suggest that such language is used for its sensationalized impact, for "tear jerk" effect, largely used to elicit donor response without providing clear information on a particular communities or grouping. It is argued that language like "urban poor"

Source:
Ripe for Harvest,
pp. 195-200

encourages over-generalization, and, using such terms to describe thousands, even millions of discrete cultures and communities is demeaning, sloppy thinking, and generally belittling to urban folk. Others suggest that such terms as "urban poor" should be replaced with other terms more sensitive to urban people, suggesting alternative phrases as "the disenfranchised" or "the economically oppressed." Some might even suggest that using any language that asserts particular differences between and among urban dwellers on the basis of class is inappropriate, and unnecessarily creates division among those whom Christ died for.

While these and related arguments have some validity, especially for those who use phrases like this in an insensitive and unthinking manner, none of them, either separate or together, disqualify the legitimate use of that term. For more than four decades as a national missions organization, World Impact has boldly identified its target population as those who reside in the city who are socio-economically poor. We use the language of "the urban poor" in this light, informed by the demographics in the city and the teaching of the Scriptures regarding God's commitment to the poor.

Poverty in the United States continues to rise. In data gathered as late as 2010, the poverty rate has been increasing to 15.1 percent in 2010 from 14.3 percent in 2009 and 13.2 percent in 2008. According to the research think-tank, the Urban Institute, there were 46.2 million poor people in 2010 compared to 43.2 million in 2009, with the poverty rater looming higher than it has been since 1993 (Urban Institute, Unemployment and Recovery Project, September 13. 2011). Sluggish job markets, high unemployment, and rising poverty rates have dramatically impacted urban communities, with literally thousands of families lacking income and access to the basic resources to live and survive. World Impact unashamedly focuses its time and attention on evangelizing, equipping, and empowering those in communities hardest hit by our recessions, economic blight, and all the by-products of violence, crime, broken family, and the overall desperation that poverty and hopelessness brings.

We do not use the term "urban poor" only to clearly identify the population to which we have been historically called. We also use the term because of the prophetic meaning of the poor in Scripture. Many dozens of text in both Old and New Testaments reveal a consistent perspective regarding God and those who are poor. They show that God has always had a burden for those who lack power, resources, money, or the necessities of life. The standards God gave to his covenant people regarding the poor reveal his commitment to the

Context
Values/Vision
Prepare
Launch
Assemble
Nurture
Transition
Schedule/Charter

Source:
Ripe for Harvest,
pp. 195-200

destitute, and all groups and classes associated with them. It is clear that the Old Testament includes a number of groups in close proximity to the poor, including orphans, widows, slaves, and the oppressed (e.g., Deut. 15; Ruth; Isa. 1). Those who exploited and took advantage of the vulnerable because of their poverty and weakness would be judged, and mercy and kindness was exhorted as the universal standard of God's people on behalf of the poor. The Law provided numerous commands regarding the fair and gracious treatment of the poor and the needy, of the demand to provide the hungry and destitute with food, and for the liberal treatment of the poor (Deut. 15.11).

The New Testament reveals God's heart for the poor crystallized in the incarnation of Jesus. Jesus proclaimed in his inaugural sermon that he was anointed with God's Spirit to proclaim the Good News of the Kingdom to the poor (Luke 4.18; 6.20), and confirmed his Messianic identity to John the Baptizer with preaching to the poor, along with healings and miracles (Luke 7.18-23). The Lord declared Zacchaeus' justice to the poor as a sign of his salvation (Luke 19.8-10), and he identified himself unequivocally with those who were sick, in prison, strangers, hungry, thirsty, and naked (Matt. 25.31-45). Every facet of Jesus' life and ministry intersected with the needs of those who lacked resources and money, and therefore could be easily exploited, oppressed, and taken advantage of.

In the actions and writings of the Apostles, we also see clear statements regarding God's election of and care for those who are economically poor. James 2.5 says that God has chosen the poor in this world to be rich in faith and to inherit the Kingdom he promised to those who love him. Paul told the Corinthians that God has chosen the foolish things of the world to shame the wise, the weak things of the world to shame the strong, the lowly and despised things of this world to nullify the things that are, in order that no one might boast in his presence (1 Cor. 1.27-29). This text and others thicken our view of the poor as merely lacking goods, services, and resources: more than that, the poor are those who need make them vulnerable to the effect of their need and the world's exploitation, and are desperate enough to rely on God's strength alone.

Context
Values/Vision
Prepare
Launch
Assemble
Nurture
Transition
Schedule/Charter

In using the term "urban poor" we make clear both the target population that guides the decisions and outreaches of our ministry, as well as unashamedly testify to the biblical perspective of God's election of and commitment to the most vulnerable, needy, and exposed people within our society. Urban dwellers outnumber all other popula-tions today, and our cities have been magnets for massive migrations of

Source:
Ripe for Harvest,
pp. 195-200

urban peoples looking for economic betterment. We believe that "empowering the urban poor" therefore is missionally strategic and prophetically potent. Missionally, the phrase is strategic because it rightly denotes the vast numbers of people who remain unreached with the Gospel of Christ who dwell in our cities. Prophetically, it is potent because it reveals our bold and unashamed call to follow in the footsteps of Jesus, our respect for the poorest of the poor, our belief that God is calling the poor to be members of his church, and our confidence that the urban poor have a significant place in raising up leaders who will reach the cities of our nation, and beyond.

What of the use of the term "urban poor" and World Impact's prayer partners and donors, and our friends and neighbors in the city? To begin with, we have used the term clearly and circumspectly to help anyone interested in our mission agency know precisely those whom God has called us to reach. We love the families and individuals that we serve in the city, and ought never use language (this phrase or any other) to shame or exploit our relationship with them. We do not use this term as a stereotyping label, some pejorative stamp to limit the potential of the communities where we live and work. Rather, we use the phrase in our materials in order to communicate clearly, forthrightly, and persuasively argue the priority of this long neglected field in evangelical mission. From the beginning we have unashamedly committed our lives and resources to making disciples and planting churches among America's urban poor. This is a stewardship, the outworking of our individual and corporate call as missionaries of Christ. God forbid that any one of us would use such language to denigrate the very ones for whom Christ died, those to whom we are called, and those which we believe are the key to future mission in America, and beyond! Speaking clearly regarding our calling is our duty, which never includes shaming or belittling any person to which we are called. For the sake of our mission, our donors, and those whom we serve, we must be unequivocal regarding our target population; likewise, we must never shame nor denigrate them in our use of any communication, ever.

"Empowering the urban poor," therefore, as our adopted language, is neither just a tag-line nor a catchy motto. Rather, for us it functions as a representation of our single vision, the integrating mission of our work as an interdenominational ministry in the city. We believe that empowerment is neither merely meeting needs, dealing only with the mere symptoms of underlying structures of poverty, nor is it being hegemonic patrons to the poor, making them forever dependent on our charity and service. As missionaries of Christ, we believe that the poor,

Source:
Ripe for Harvest,
pp. 195-200

like any other people, can be redeemed, transformed, and released to be the people of God in their own communities. When God wanted to empower his people, he sent his Holy Spirit upon the apostolic company, and formed a community which he entrusted with the life of God and the Word of life. The answer of God to systemic poverty and neglect was to form a people who embodied the very life of the Kingdom where freedom, wholeness, and justice reside. These communities are entrusted with a mission to gather the elect from among the poorest, most broken people on earth, and, through the power of the Spirit and Christian community, see the Kingdom come to earth in new relationships of hospitality, generosity, and righteousness, right where they live. Every healthy functioning church is an outpost of the Kingdom of God, and can be a place where true transformation takes place. Nothing "empowers" the poor like a simple assembly of believers, obedient to the Lordship of Christ!

Armed with this perspective, we wholeheartedly believe that no organization in the history of the world can recognize the dignity and value of the poor like the Church of Jesus Christ. In light of this conviction, World Impact strives to plant as many churches as fast as possible among the various cultures represented by the urban poor, in all of our cities and beyond. We are convinced that no other social organization has the endorsement of God, the headship of Christ, and the power of the Spirit like a healthy functioning local church. And, nothing empowers a community like facilitating church planting movements among the urban poor, where the life and power of the Gospel of Christ can reach and transform entire communities as outposts of the Kingdom. All that we do in mission and in justice (from our camps, our schools, our businesses, medical and dental clinics, our work in the jails and the prisons, and most important of all, our missionary church planting and leadership development efforts) contribute to this empowerment work. Rather than merely meet needs or serve as patrons to the poor, we believe that the Spirit of God can win them, raise up leaders, empower them to lead, and release them as laborers in their very own communities as ambassadors of Christ. More than being recipients of care, we believe they can receive investment to be God's servant leaders, transformers of their communities and co-laborers in God's Kingdom work.

In conclusion, while the phrase "empowering the urban poor" may be misused and misapplied, we at World Impact wholeheartedly embrace the phrase not only because it clarifies the target population of our mission, but also because it unequivocally states our prophetic call to represent God's unchanging commitment to the most vulnerable and least resourced among us. Let us allow Jesus' challenge given so

Context
Values/Vision
Prepare
Launch
Assemble
Nurture
Transition
Schedule/Charter

Source:
Ripe for Harvest,
pp. 195-200

many centuries ago to continue to be our model and vision of ministry today as we seek to fulfill the Great Commission among the world's urban poor:

> Then the King will say to those on his right, "Come, you who are blessed by my Father, inherit the kingdom prepared for you from the foundation of the world. For I was hungry and you gave me food, I was thirsty and you gave me drink, I was a stranger and you welcomed me, I was naked and you clothed me, I was sick and you visited me, I was in prison and you came to me." Then the righteous will answer him, saying, "Lord, when did we see you hungry and feed you, or thirsty and give you drink? And when did we see you a stranger and welcome you, or naked and clothe you? And when did we see you sick or in prison and visit you?" And the King will answer them, "Truly, I say to you, as you did it to one of the least of these my brothers, you did it to me."
>
> ~ Matthew 25.34-40 (ESV)

Context
Values/Vision
Prepare
Launch
Assemble
Nurture
Transition
Schedule/Charter

SEMINAR 2
Church Planting Overview
Rev. Dr. Don L. Davis

Source:
Ripe for Harvest,
pp. 54-64

How to PLANT a Church

I. Overview

    A. Evangelize, equip, empower

    B. PLANT

        1. Prepare: Be the Church

        2. Launch: Expand the Church

        3. Assemble: Establish the Church

        4. Nurture: Mature the Church

        5. Transition: Release the Church

    C. The steps

        1. Evangelize: Prepare, Launch

        2. Equip: Assemble, Nurture

        3. Empower: Transition

Context
Values/Vision
Prepare
Launch
Assemble
Nurture
Transition
Schedule/Charter

Evangelize

Source:
Ripe for Harvest,
pp. 54-64

Mark 16.15-18 (ESV) – And he said to them, "Go into all the world and proclaim the gospel to the whole creation. [16] Whoever believes and is baptized will be saved, but whoever does not believe will be condemned. [17] And these signs will accompany those who believe: in my name they will cast out demons; they will speak in new tongues; [18] they will pick up serpents with their hands; and if they drink any deadly poison, it will not hurt them; they will lay their hands on the sick, and they will recover."

II. Prepare: Be the Church

Acts 16.25 (ESV) - About midnight Paul and Silas were praying and singing hymns to God, and the prisoners were listening to them.

A. Principle: A church is birthed from an existing church (we have to BE the church before we can plant the church).

1. We reproduce after our own kind. We do not start churches *ex nihilo*, but from other churches. We have an organic link from church to church back to Pentecost; to the Apostles; to Israel; to the Trinity. Community has been eternally existent; we are a part of that stream.

2. As in families, parents birth children, raise them in their homes and prepare them to be parents. Offspring bear our name and character. They share our biology and nurture. This intimacy is needed to create and sustain a church-planting movement. We do not distinguish the spirituality of training leaders from the spirituality of cross-cultural church planters.

3. New congregations will share our vision, doctrine, spiritual discipline, mission and finances. There is no distinction between the new congregation and the sent team.

4. The "P" of PLANT recognizes that the church exists as soon as the team is formed. Paul's team WAS the church in Philippi before Lydia's household joined them. Launch simply adds to the existing church.

Context
Values/Vision
Prepare
Launch
Assemble
Nurture
Transition
Schedule/Charter

Source:
Ripe for Harvest,
pp. 54-64

B. Elements of Prepare

1. Seek God's leading to select an unchurched target area or population (which may include demographic and ethnographic studies).

2. Form a church-plant team, the initial church which community believers can join.

3. Select a reproducible model to contextualize standard Church practices.

4. Initiate discussions about associations, denominations or other affiliations.

III. Launch: Expand the Church

Acts 2.47 (ESV) - And the Lord added to their number day by day those who were being saved.

A. Principle: Begin inviting people to join the community

B. Elements of Launch

1. Invite others (mature or new believers) to join the church.

2. Conduct evangelism to add to the existing church.

3. Follow up new converts

Context
Values/Vision
Prepare
Launch
Assemble
Nurture
Transition
Schedule/Charter

Equip

Source:
Ripe for Harvest,
pp. 54-64

> Eph. 4.11-16 (ESV) – And he gave the apostles, the prophets, the evangelists, the pastors and teachers, [12] to equip the saints for the work of ministry, for building up the body of Christ, [13] until we all attain to the unity of the faith and of the knowledge of the Son of God, to mature manhood, to the measure of the stature of the fullness of Christ, [14] so that we may no longer be children, tossed to and fro by the waves and carried about by every wind of doctrine, by human cunning, by craftiness in deceitful schemes. [15] Rather, speaking the truth in love, we are to grow up in every way into him who is the head, into Christ, [16] from whom the whole body, joined and held together by every joint with which it is equipped, when each part is working properly, makes the body grow so that it builds itself up in love.

IV. Assemble: Establish the Church

Heb. 10.25 (ESV) - not neglecting to meet together, as is the habit of some, but encouraging one another, and all the more as you see the Day drawing near.

A. Principle: Bring the church to a place where it can be announced in the community as a functioning Body.

B. Elements of Assemble

   1. Train others through cell groups or Bible studies to follow up and disciple new believers.

   2. Continue evangelism with *oikos* groups.

   3. Identify and train emerging leaders, focusing on preparing leaders for Transition at a satellite campus of The Urban Ministry Institute (TUMI).

   4. Assemble the groups where the Word is rightly preached, the sacraments are rightly administered and discipline is rightly ordered.

   5. Announce to the neighborhood the beginning of public worship.

Context
Values/Vision
Prepare
Launch
Assemble
Nurture
Transition
Schedule/Charter

Source:
Ripe for Harvest,
pp. 54-64

V. Nurture: Mature the Church

1 Pet. 4.10 (ESV) - As each has received a gift, use it to serve one another, as good stewards of God's varied grace.

A. Principle: Leaders observe and practice their developing skills in a church with real people, identities and structures, under leadership that ensures consistent practices.

1. Leaders must be developed in the context of community, using the same theological, strategic, and Church practices that ensure replication from one church to another. For example, when an emerging leader learns how to serve communion at the mother church, s/he knows how to lead communion at the daughter church plant.

2. The contextualization of the standard Church practices must be designed to make it easy to train leaders and export to new churches. Structures facilitate and enable innovation.

B. Elements of Nurture

1. Use the Church Year calendar to disciple the congregation.

2. Train others to serve and lead through individual and group discipleship.

3. Encourage believers to exercise their gifts in the church.

4. Assign responsibility to the faithful (deacons, elders, future pastors).

Context
Values/Vision
Prepare
Launch
Assemble
Nurture
Transition
Schedule/Charter

Empower

Source:
Ripe for Harvest,
pp. 54-64

Acts 20.28 (ESV) – Pay careful attention to yourselves and to all the flock, in which the Holy Spirit has made you overseers, to care for the church of God, which he obtained with his own blood.

Acts 20.32 (ESV) – And now I commend you to God and to the word of his grace, which is able to build you up and to give you the inheritance among all those who are sanctified.

VI. Transition: Release the Church

2 Tim. 2.2 (ESV) - and what you have heard from me in the presence of many witnesses entrust to faithful men who will be able to teach others also.

A. Principle: Make ready the release of cross-cultural church planters to pass the baton to indigenous leadership.

B. Elements of Transition

1. Commission faithful indigenous leaders to be deacons, elders and pastors.

2. Commission the church to be part of a self-governing, self-supporting and self-reproducing movement.

3. Join a denomination or association for fellowship, support and joint-ministry activity.

4. Begin reproducing a new church plant.

Evangelize

PREPARE: Be the Church

- Seek God's leading to select an unchurched target area or population.
- Form a church-plant team, the initial church which community believers can join.
- Select a reproducible model to contextualize standard Church practices.
- Initiate discussions about associations, denominations or other affiliations.

Source:
Ripe for Harvest,
pp. 54-64

LAUNCH: Expand the Church

- Invite others (mature or new believers) to join the church.

- Conduct evangelism to add to the existing church.

- Follow up new converts using "Fight the Good Fight of Faith."

Equip

ASSEMBLE: Establish the Church

- Train others through cell groups or Bible studies to follow up and disciple new believers.

- Continue evangelism with *oikos* groups.

- Identify and train emerging leaders at a satellite campus of TUMI.

- Assemble the groups where the Word is rightly preached, the sacraments are rightly administered and discipline is rightly ordered.

- Announce to the neighborhood the beginning of public worship.

NURTURE: Mature the Church

- Use the Church Year calendar to disciple the congregation.

- Train others to serve and lead through individual and group discipleship.

- Encourage believers to exercise their gifts in the church.

- Assign responsibility to the faithful (deacons, elders, future pastors).

Empower

TRANSITION: Release the Church

- Commission faithful indigenous leaders to be deacons, elders and pastors.

- Commission the church to be part of a self-governing, self-supporting and self-reproducing movement.

- Join a denomination or association for fellowship, support and joint-ministry activity.

- Begin reproducing a new church plant.

Context
Values/Vision
Prepare
Launch
Assemble
Nurture
Transition
Schedule/Charter

Source:
Ripe for Harvest,
pp. 54-64

Pauline Precedents from Acts: The Pauline Cycle

1. Missionaries Commissioned: Acts 13.1-4; 15.39-40; Gal. 1.15-16.

2. Audience Contacted: Acts 13.14-16; 14.1; 16.13-15; 17.16-19.

3. Gospel Communicated: Acts 13.17-41; 16.31; Rom. 10.9-14; 2 Tim. 2.8.

4. Hearers Converted: Acts. 13.48; 16.14-15; 20.21; 26.20; 1 Thess. 1.9-10.

5. Believers Congregated: Acts 13.43; 19.9; Rom 16.4-5; 1 Cor. 14.26.

6. Faith Confirmed: Acts 14.21-22; 15.41; Rom 16.17; Col. 1.28; 2 Thess. 2.15; 1 Tim. 1.3.

7. Leadership Consecrated; Acts 14.23; 2 Tim. 2.2; Titus 1.5.

8. Believers Commended; Acts 14.23; 16.40; 21.32 (2 Tim. 4.9 and Titus 3.12 by implication).

9. Relationships Continued: Acts 15.36; 18.23; 1 Cor. 16.5; Eph. 6.21-22; Col. 4.7-8.

10. Sending Churches Convened: Acts 14.26-27; 15.1-4.

The "Pauline Cycle" terminology, stages, and diagram are taken from David J. Hesselgrave, *Planting Churches Cross-Culturally,* 2nd ed. Grand Rapids: Baker Book House, 2000.

"Evangelize, Equip, and Empower" and "P.L.A.N.T." schemas for church planting taken from *Crowns of Beauty: Planting Urban Churches Conference Binder* Los Angeles: World Impact Press, 1999.

**Context
Values/Vision**
Prepare
Launch
Assemble
Nurture
Transition
Schedule/Charter

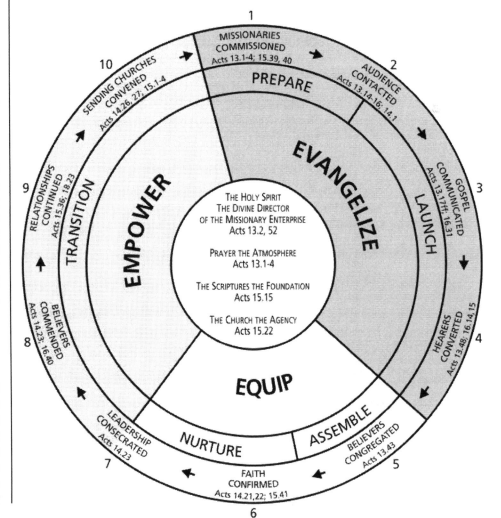

Source:
Ripe for Harvest,
pp. 54-64

Ten Principles of Church Planting

1. **Jesus is Lord.** (Matt. 9.37-38) All church plant activity is made effective and fruitful under the watch care and power of the Lord Jesus, who himself is the Lord of the harvest.

2. **Evangelize, Equip, and Empower unreached people to reach people.** (1 Thess. 1.6-8) Our goal in reaching others for Christ is not only for solid conversion but also for dynamic multiplication; those who are reached must be trained to reach others as well.

3. **Be inclusive: whosoever will may come.** (Rom. 10.12) No strategy should forbid any person or group from entering into the Kingdom through Jesus Christ by faith.

4. **Be culturally neutral: Come just as you are.** (Col. 3.11) The Gospel places no demands on any seeker to change their culture as a prerequisite for coming to Jesus; they may come just as they are.

5. **Avoid a fortress mentality.** (Acts 1.8) The goal of missions is not to create an impregnable castle in the midst of an unsaved community, but a dynamic outpost of the Kingdom which launches a witness for Jesus within and unto the very borders of their world.

6. **Continue to evangelize to avoid stagnation.** (Rom. 1.16-17) Keep looking to the horizons with the vision of the Great Commission in mind; foster an environment of aggressive witness for Christ.

7. **Cross racial, class, gender, and language barriers.** (1 Cor. 9.19-22) Use your freedom in Christ to find new, credible ways to communicate the kingdom message to those farthest from the cultural spectrum of the traditional church.

8. **Respect the dominance of the receiving culture.** (Acts 15.23-29) Allow the Holy Spirit to incarnate the vision and the ethics of the Kingdom of God in the words, language, customs, styles, and experience of those who have embraced Jesus as their Lord.

9. **Avoid dependence.** (Eph. 4.11-16) Neither patronize nor be overly stingy towards the growing congregation; do not underestimate the power of the Spirit in the midst of even the smallest Christian community to accomplish God's work in their community.

10. **Think reproducibility.** (2 Tim. 2.2; Phil. 1.18) In every activity and project you initiate, think in terms of equipping others to do the same by maintaining an open mind regarding the means and ends of your missionary endeavors.

**Context
Values/Vision**
Prepare
Launch
Assemble
Nurture
Transition
Schedule/Charter

Input, Process, Results

Dave Klopfenstein

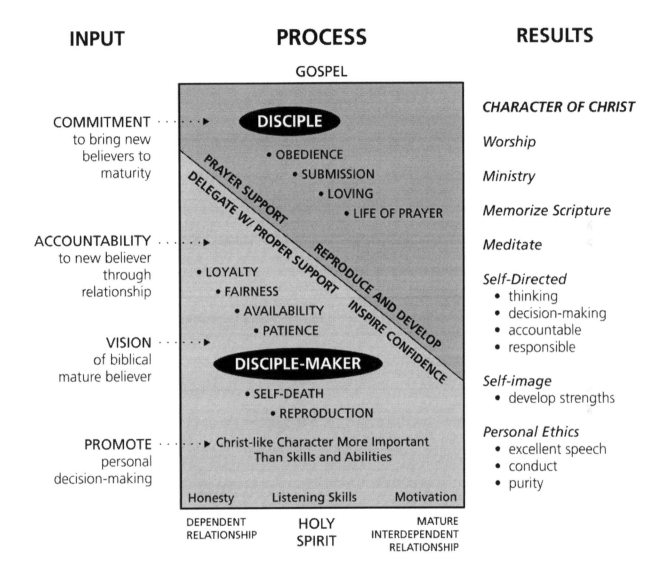

INPUT	PROCESS	RESULTS

PROCESS — GOSPEL

DISCIPLE
- OBEDIENCE
- SUBMISSION
- LOVING
- LIFE OF PRAYER

PRAYER SUPPORT
DELEGATE W/ PROPER SUPPORT
REPRODUCE AND DEVELOP
INSPIRE CONFIDENCE

- LOYALTY
- FAIRNESS
- AVAILABILITY
- PATIENCE

DISCIPLE-MAKER
- SELF-DEATH
- REPRODUCTION

Christ-like Character More Important Than Skills and Abilities

Honesty   Listening Skills   Motivation

DEPENDENT RELATIONSHIP   HOLY SPIRIT   MATURE INTERDEPENDENT RELATIONSHIP

INPUT

COMMITMENT
to bring new believers to maturity

ACCOUNTABILITY
to new believer through relationship

VISION
of biblical mature believer

PROMOTE
personal decision-making

RESULTS

CHARACTER OF CHRIST

Worship

Ministry

Memorize Scripture

Meditate

Self-Directed
- thinking
- decision-making
- accountable
- responsible

Self-image
- develop strengths

Personal Ethics
- excellent speech
- conduct
- purity

Source: *Ripe for Harvest,* pp. 54-64

Source:
Ripe for Harvest,
pp. 54-64

Review the following appendices in *Planting Churches among the City's Poor: An Anthology of Urban Church Planting Resources* (please refer to the Appendix Table at the end of this session in order to find the location of each document listed below, i.e., its volume and page number), and then answer together the questions under *Seminar Group Discussion*.

- Church Planting Models
- The Nature of Dynamic Church Planting Movements
- The Threefold Cord of Urban Cross-Cultural Church Planting Movements
- Church Planting Movements, C1 Neighborhoods, and 80% Windows: The Importance of Vision
- Forming the Church Plant Team and Understanding the Roles

Seminar Group Discussion

1. Explain briefly the key components of the concepts of EEE and PLANT.
2. How does the PLANT acrostic help us understand the basic NT apostolic approaches to planting churches among the lost?
3. Briefly explain the various church plant models being employed today, and discuss their implications for planting churches among the poor in the city.
4. How does the World Impact language of expressions help us better understand how we can think of authentic Christian assembly, apart from the model language?

Context
Values/Vision
Prepare
Launch
Assemble
Nurture
Transition
Schedule/Charter

Source:
Ripe for Harvest,
pp. 90-92

What Is a Church?

Rev. Dr. Don Davis

The Church is the community of God's people who acknowledge Jesus as Lord, who carry out his purposes on earth, comprised of everyone past, present and future, from every place on the earth and throughout history. The Church is God's agent of the Kingdom of God, the body and bride of Christ, who as custodian of God's revelation has responded to his work in theology, worship, discipleship and witness (see *The Story of God: Our Sacred Roots*). Each local church is an embassy, serving as an outpost of his Kingdom.

There is a single story revealed in the Bible (see *Once Upon a Time*). The God of the universe, existing in three Persons (Father, Son, and Holy Spirit), is the Creator of all things, visible and invisible, who made human beings in His own image. Despite the rebellion of Satan and the first human pair, God sent a Savior who would overcome evil and win everything back for the glory of God.

In this unfolding drama, there is an objective foundation (the sovereign work of God in creation, Israel, and Christ) and a subjective response (the Church's participation in God's Kingdom). On the objective side, the Father is the Author and Director of the Story, the Son is the Champion and Lead Actor of the Story, and the Spirit is the Narrator and Interpreter of the Story. The Bible is the Script and Testimony of the Story.

On the subjective side, the People of the Story respond in orthodox theology as confessors of the faith, worship together as royal priests, are formed as disciples of Christ as sojourners in this world, and witness to God's love as his holy ambassadors. This understanding creates the foundation for every expression in a local church (see *Christus Victor: An Integrated Vision for the Christian Life and Witness*) including doctrine, use of gifts, spirituality, justice and compassion, evangelism and mission, and worship.

The Church is called to faithfully embody and defend God's revelation through the apostle's testimony, fulfilling its identity as one, holy, universal, and apostolic community (see *There Is a River*). The Church is to faithfully pass down what the Spirit gave to Christ's people in terms of what they believe, how they are to worship, and what their Scriptures would be. These foundational beliefs undergird the faith for all believers, everywhere, and is called the "Great Tradition" (see *The Nicene Creed*) which is embraced by all orthodox believers. This represents the teaching and practice of the apostles, written in the Bible, summarized

**Context
Values/Vision**
Prepare
Launch
Assemble
Nurture
Transition
Schedule/Charter

Source:
Ripe for Harvest,
pp. 90-92

in the creeds and councils of the Church, and defended by believers throughout history.

Church planting is simply an extension of the subjective expression of this Grand Cosmic Drama. A church plant is a new leaf on the Tree of God's design, going back to its Sacred Roots. Our identity is based on the guardianship and cross-cultural transference of the Great Tradition, which guards against heresy, sectarianism, syncretism, schism and pragmatism.

Once we see the broad landscape of the Church (big "C") we can then think more responsibly and clearly about the church (little "c"). In World Impact's conceptual dictionary, we acknowledge that the Church has historically and practically today expressed its community in three ways. These expressions will prove to be essential in our outworking of church planting among city folk, and encompasses all facets of our church planting strategy (including assessment for church planters, training and chartering church plant teams, and providing resources and directions through our coaches and funding).

(The purposes of these expressions is not to determine the absolute line between, say, 50 and 51 members in a church. Obviously, these numbers are not given for hard-and-fast distinctions between expressions. Rather, the numbers are meant to help provide us with a sense of the congregations regular, ongoing, size and makeup. Churches breathe in their membership, but do tend to settle at a particular attendance within margins. Do not see the numbers as absolute boundaries but rather as suggestive guidelines in terms of how a particular church tends to grow and function.)

Our three expressions are as follows:

The Small Church (or "house church," 20-50 or so people).
The small (or house) church can be understood as a *small store in a shopping mall*. It needs the connections to other small churches to both survive and thrive. Small churches are able to meet virtually anywhere and can operate with a tiny footprint with little to no financial burdens. They can focus on a specific block, housing development, or network of families. This expression allows for a strong discipleship focus of indigenous leadership development which can take place in this smaller connected group.

Community Church (60-150 or so people)
The community church is the most common expression of church, numerically speaking, in the world today. This expression can be understood as a *grocery or convenience store in a neighborhood or*

Source:
Ripe for Harvest,
pp. 90-92

community. This expression focuses on a particular geographic identity and proximity, highlighting the affinity, connection, and unique context of the congregation and the surrounding community. It is developed around a deep calling and connection to a particular neighborhood, and typically requires a semi-stable place to meet (e.g., a park, community center, or school). This expression especially depends on and is enriched by explicit partnerships formed with other community churches, which effectively strengthens and feeds their growth and mission as individual assemblies.

Mother Church (200+ people)

The mother church (or "hub church") represents a larger assembly of believers, and can be understood as *a Walmart Superstore or Super Target, a store which houses a number of select entities that supply its patrons with many choices and opportunities.* This kind of church, which has both the economic and spiritual resources for multiplication, can leverage its resources and capabilities to become both a sending/empowering church which reproduces itself many times over. Ideally, a mother or hub church is a congregation that is lead by clear missional intents that allow it to leverage its capabilities and gifts to become a center of compassion, mercy, and justice ministries. It can also come to serve as the nurturing headquarters for church planters and ministry starters, and can easily operate as an incubator of other effective ministries among the unreached urban poor. Such an expression usually is more rooted in a particular built-to-suit facility that allows it to leverage these kinds of capabilities.

Context
Values/Vision
Prepare
Launch
Assemble
Nurture
Transition
Schedule/Charter

Summary of Key Cross-Cultural Church Planting Principles

World Impact

1. Jesus is Lord.

The cardinal principle in church planting is that Jesus of Nazareth has been raised to the position of God's heir and Lord of the Church and the Harvest (Matt. 28.18-20; Heb. 1.1-4). Nothing that takes place in the Church, in mission, or in the spiritual realm has any lasting meaning or power without the sovereignty and overseership of Jesus Christ, who has been granted authority and a name which all creatures everywhere will one day acknowledge and worship (cf. Phil. 2.5-11). An understanding that Jesus is Lord, working through the Holy Spirit in this age to accomplish all that He has determined is the foundation and rock upon which all who minister must reckon and receive (i.e., Acts 1.8; John 14.16-17). No church plant team operates in an isolated manner, divorced from God's power, influence, leading, and resources. Because Jesus is Lord, we can now go and make disciples among all the people groups He has called us to minister to, and do so with the full assurance that He will remain with us at every phase of the plant, even until the very end of the age (Matt. 28.20).

2. Evangelize, equip, and empower unreached people to reach people.

God's intent is to draw out of the earth a people that will forever belong to Him through the covenant promise made to Abraham and ratified through Abraham's seed, the Lord Jesus Christ. As a result, we know that God has commanded His Church to go into the entire world, preaching the Good News of His grace and Kingdom throughout the earth. This command is for everyone, and for those who repent and believe, becoming members of His family and church, they are given the high privilege to represent Him as well. Those whom we evangelize, follow-up, and disciple in the city are also called to become His witnesses, and join us in winning their friends, families, and neighbors to the Lord Jesus. Our intent, therefore, in mission, is not merely to win others, but to see God so mature His Church among the urban poor that they become empowered to join us as colleagues in winning their surrounding cities and neighborhoods to Jesus Christ as well (cf. Col. 1.27-29; Eph. 4.9-16; 1 Pet. 3.15).

3. Be inclusive; whosoever will may come.

The command of Jesus is given to all, that is, His offer of forgiveness and redemption is universal in scope, bringing life and grace to all who believe (e.g., John 1.12-13; 3.16; 5.24; 10.27-29; 1 John 5.11-13, etc.). Therefore, God is now commanding all people everywhere to repent and believe in His Son (Acts 17.30-31), and bids them to come to Him whatever their station in life, color, class, gender, race, or background. The grace of God that appears to all of us is a free, unmerited, and universal grace that is not bounded or limited in any way to a person's culture, clan, country, or circumstance. The universality of the Gospel is one of the most significant principles related to its dynamism and vitality. By failing to be inclusive, we can easily make our so-called "evangelistic outreach" just one more attempt to engage in a kind of spiritual social engineering where the deserving get to hear of Jesus' Good News, and the unlovely and undeserving others are ignored or spurned. Let your church planting efforts be known for your zeal to get the Word of God to all of those in the area where God has placed you, and to all of them to whom He has called (cf. Gal. 2.6-10).

4. Be culturally neutral: come just as you are.

In Jesus Christ there is no Jew nor Greek, male nor female, barbarian, Scythian, slave, free, Black, White, or whatever. When we engage in church planting we acknowledge that the grace of God is universal in scope, that no one culture can claim any special status or place, that individuals are called to become disciples of Jesus in the midst of their own cultures, and that God welcomes them as they are, without regard to their cultural or racial history (Acts 10, 11). The concept of cultural neutrality simply means that the Gospel does not pick and choose among the peoples of the world as to which ones are deserving, more holy, more morally fit, or better spiritually suited to hear the Good News of Jesus Christ. Our intent is to share the Gospel with all of the clarity and love that Christ's call has constrained upon us, but never to be impartial or prejudiced in our offering or demonstration of the Gospel (cf. James 2.1-9). God commands us to speak the Good News of Christ's deliverance to all peoples, regardless of their cultures, who can come to Him in the midst of their own culture, and among whom the Holy Spirit can plant a church which represents a branch of God's holy people *in the very heart* of the culture itself. No person of a particular culture needs to change their culture in order to be born from above, and live as a disciple of Jesus Christ, for, in regards to the Kingdom of God, what Paul says is absolutely true; "Christ is all, and in all" (Col. 3.11).

5. Avoid a fortress mentality.

In planting a church in the city among the poor, there will be a new, supernatural impulse to create through your outreach and the church and its programs, a haven of help and hope for the numerous issues, problems, and challenges that the believers in these communities face. This is the very nature of the substance of true spirituality: to demonstrate the love of God practically among those who have need (cf. 1 John 4.7-8).

While we ought to strive to demonstrate practically the love and justice of the Kingdom of Christ through our ministries, we must also avoid the tendency to make our programs, outreaches, and activities at our preaching points or outreach neighborhoods a kind of ends-in-themselves. A "fortress mentality" is that tendency of ministry in the city where we make our particular efforts in a specific target community the "all-in-all" of ministry itself, and our proverbial efforts become a kind of "little kingdom on the corner" where all our time, attention, and efforts are linked to the programs we host and sponsor there. The heart of the Kingdom message is advancing and taking the Good News to those who have not heard of Jesus yet (Rom. 15.20-21). No church plant must be seen as an end in itself, but as another outpost of the Kingdom whereby the Good News can be sent to neighboring communities which need to hear of God's love.

6. Continue to evangelize to avoid stagnation.

As we begin to harvest the fruit of the proclamation of the Word of God, and start to give much of our time and attention to the nurture and equipping of the new believers, it is important that we do not lose our momentum in evangelism. Not only are new believers often times some of the best soul winners in the Church, it is important to emphasize sharing the Good News with the lost lest we fall prey to the common tendency of the "Jesus and us only" syndrome. Attending to the needs of our emerging flocks, (even the smallest ones!) can easily eclipse our responsibility to not only do critical "inreach" within the body (e.g., providing teaching, fellowship, worship, and tender loving care to the members) but also to continue to do "outreach" to the lost and hurting around us (e.g., evangelism, ministering, and serving the broken in our community, etc.). In order to avoid the kind of numbing stagnation that can come from being self-focused, we ought to emphasize within the emerging church from the very beginning its ongoing responsibility to be light and salt to their neighbors, sharing the Good News of Jesus with their family, friends, and associates.

7. Cross racial, class, gender and language barriers.

The soul of cross-cultural church planting is being led and empowered by the Holy Spirit and Jesus' leading to cross barriers in order to win and disciple people into the Church. In other words, church planting in the city will involve developing timely and wise strategies to identify the barriers that urbanites are facing in hearing the Good News, and making specific plans to transcend these barriers in order that the members of a specific and targeted population can hear the Gospel communicated in their own native language, and be given the opportunity to grow and mature in Christ in sync with and in the midst of their own people and culture. Of course, it will require much prayer in helping believers understand the difference between those elements in their culture which are immoral (contrary to the values of the Kingdom of God), moral (consistent with the values of the Kingdom of God), and amoral (practices which do not have any moral significance, but are simply issues of preferences and taste). As Paul suggests, we are to become all things to all people in order to win some (i.e., 1 Cor. 9.22-27), meaning that we are to teach believers how to live free in Christ, but not to use their freedom as a covering or a license for sin but to express with honor and holiness their love for Jesus in the midst of their own people and cultural group (1 Pet. 2.16; Gal. 5.1,11). We cross the barriers to make the Gospel plain so people can respond to Christ intelligently and cogently; the Gospel is for the Jew and the Greek (Rom. 1.16-17).

8. Respect the dominance of the receiving culture.

In all phases of our activities and outreaches, we are to respect the dominance of the culture in which God has placed us, for the purpose of making disciples. In other words, we ought to avoid having the members of another people group conform to our norms of culture as they define and express their own sense of life in Christ. We ought to expect that the culture will express and respond to God and His leading in unique and different ways, very much unlike our own, or even from the ways of "traditional" Christian practice. This orientation is simply an acknowledgment of the freedom that the receiving culture has in following Christ as the Holy Spirit leads them, and not necessarily in the same way and manner in which you personally or your team is either familiar or comfortable with. Recall the shock and horror of Peter and his team to the falling of the Holy Spirit on Cornelius and the rest of his Gentile clan (Acts 10-11)! The apostles refused to place upon the Gentiles any extra burden regarding their discipleship except "to abstain from the pollutions of idols and from unchastity and from what is strangled and from blood" (Acts 15.20, RSV). In all our evangelism, disciple making, and church planting, we ought to believe that the Holy Spirit will work in and through the receiving culture in ways different and even beyond our own.

9. Avoid dependence.

In a real sense, fledgling urban churches, once they begin, are like children. They need the kind of constant, creative, and concerned care that any infant needs, and, in the same way, need this input around the clock. It is only natural for us to want to provide for the needs of the burgeoning church, and help it to avoid all the mistakes, problems, and challenges they will necessarily face. Sometimes, in an effort to stand with and support the growing church, church planters make the mistake of being paternalistic and patronizing to them, that is, the error of interfering with the new church's need to trust and depend on God for its resources and direction. God's intent for the church is not that we do the work for them, but that we equip the members to do the work of the ministry in order that the church might grow to become mature to the measure of Jesus' very own stature, growing both in numbers (as God leads) and in maturity (through the Holy Spirit) (Eph. 4.15-16). We are called as spiritual parents to lay up for them as children, and yet not interfere or cause an unduly and unnecessary dependence upon us and our resources for their well-being and leading. This demands discernment; too much supply and we can take the place of the Holy Spirit. On the other hand, by taking this principle to the extreme on the other end we may become stingy and mean-spirited to the little community, all the while saying it is for their sakes that we provide them with so little support or aid. We must understand that a church plant process for a community is a series of stages helping the new community move from its natural early dependence upon us, toward independence as a strong church, to interdependence as a partner with us in Kingdom mission. Helping a new community matriculate through this threefold process is the heart of the urban church planter's enterprise.

10. Think reproducibility.

As mentioned above, the Great Commission is a global mandate, involving the challenge of making disciples among all the unreached peoples of the world (Matt. 28.18-20). While simply adding a new Christian community here and there throughout our urban centers is a wonderful task, we are called to multiplication, to seeing the Good News spread throughout the entire earth, starting from our own "Jerusalems," and continuing on to our neighboring "Samarias" and to "the ends of the earth" (Acts 1.8). Our intent must be to see the churches that we plant become reproducing churches, and we must work and pray that this vision and burden be inculcated within the very DNA of the plant. In order to accomplish this goal, we must "think reproducibility," that is we must ponder how we can practically equip those Christians in the receiving culture to share the Good News of Christ with others as soon as they possibly can. We must seek creative and innovative ways to help these believers to be freed up to embrace the Great Commission as their own, and challenge them to become vessels of the Gospel advance as quickly as possible. We ought to avoid burdening them with processes and suggestions that will tie them to huge, unmanageable structures, and resist all temptations to link them to practices and activities which cannot be transferred or translated easily. In all our training and equipping we ought to emphasize simple, biblical, and reproducible models of evangelism and discipleship, and suggest workable structures and processes that will allow them to join us in ministering to the city as quickly as possible. In all our teaching and prayer, our motto and mantra must be to enable them to become our ministry partners as soon as possible, so the very momentum of the Kingdom advance can be felt from the first day of our evangelism and outreach. Let us put nothing in the path of the growing Christians and new churches which will prevent the Holy Spirit from allowing our church plants to become the start of unique movements of reproducing, vital congregations, all of which are committed to using their talents, time, and treasure to advance the Kingdom's cause throughout their neighborhoods, their city, and from them in their neighborhoods, even to "the ends of the earth."

Made in the USA
Middletown, DE
21 October 2017

This important collection of writings is taken from the official packet of church planting reference materials made available to every participant in our Evangel School of Urban Church Planting event. We selected these writings in order to help coaches and church planters understand the fundamental issues associated with planting a church in a particular context. Whatever role you play in the church planting process, these articles will help inform and orient you to the critical concepts, processes, and overall vision and strategy of church planting in general, and our Evangel training sessions in particular. So, whether you are a candidate to lead an Evangel School, a coach of a church plant leader and team, or planting a church yourself, you are sure to benefit greatly by a careful consideration of these materials. These church planting insights are truly the "front matters" you should be aware of before you engage in the rewarding ministry of church planting.

World Impact is a Christian missions organization committed to facilitating church-planting movements by evangelizing, equipping, and empowering the unchurched urban poor.

The Urban Ministry Institute (TUMI), its research arm, equips leaders and empowers movements for the same end.

www.tumi.org
www.worldimpact.org

ISBN 9781629323084

90000 >

9 781629 323084

equipping leaders.
empowering movements.

TRANSFORMING COMMUNITIES TOGETHER

W3-BAZ-824

The Urban Ministry Institute is a ministry of World Impact, Inc.

"Wait a minute!" cried the ermine. "How will we present such a gift to the newborn Babe?"

Arc-y said, "Choose several members from your group to bring the message of your gift to the Christ Child."

A vote was taken and the ermine, fox, Arctic hare and ptarmigan were chosen to bring the news of their gift to Bethlehem.

The four messengers left for the distant Bethlehem, and the remaining animals returned home. They retired to their beds for welcome rests after the exciting day.

As the animals slept, Arc-y gift-wrapped each of the sleeping animals in a blanket of newly fallen snow.

Meanwhile, the four messengers made the long journey to Bethlehem. The star that marked the manger site grew brighter and brighter. The animals became very excited. Soon the stable was in view.

As the four messengers traveled through the dark night, their journey almost over, the Arctic hare screamed in surprise, "Why, look at us! We have changed color."

"We have beautiful new coats," cried the ermine.

"They are so white that, even in the darkness, we can be seen," said the ptarmigan.

"A gift from the Arctic Angel, no doubt," murmured the wise Arctic fox. "Arc-y wanted us looking our best as we delivered our gift to the special child."

The four messengers did indeed look their best. The ptarmigan's feathers were dazzling white. The dull brown and tan fur of the remaining three messengers had also been changed into the purest white.

"Let us deliver the 'perfect' gift to the Christ Child," said the fox. So, in their new white dress, the four messengers proudly presented their gift to the Christ Child.....

themselves.

Author's Biography

Michael J. Larson taught high school biology for thirty-four years. That's when he encountered the animals of the tundra for the first time. In the beginning they were subjects in ecology presentations to his students. Then he included them in a Christmas story written for an environmental column in a small monthly farm newspaper over twenty-five years ago. The author resurrected that Christmas column one year later re-writing it as a children's story and "Nature's Christmas Story" was born!

Mr. Larson first wrote for children when he produced an environmental column for the magazine "Minnesota out of Doors", St. Paul, Minnesota. He later published the seventy-two columns resulting from the six year writing stint into a three volume collection titled "Children in the Outdoors".

Although he is retired from full time teaching he continues to develop environmental learning experiences for children as the director of the Bonanza Education Center along Big Stone Lake several miles south of Beardsley, Minnesota.

The author lives with his wife Kathie on a small acreage near the town of Wheaton, Minnesota. They have three grown children who have blessed the family with seven grandchildren.

Illustrator's Biography

Janine Ringdahl Schmidt grew up in a family that supported and encouraged her art interests. It was always her dream to be an artist.

After graduating from Wheaton High School, Janine attended the Minneapolis College of Art and Design. She graduated in 1989 with a Bachelor of Fine Arts Degree.

Following graduation she worked as a freelance artist doing both graphic design and illustration.

In 1990 she returned to her hometown and married Alan Schmidt. Her art experience expanded as she added custom painting of children's furniture and teaching local art classes to her resume.

She and her husband have three children, Hannah, age fifteen; Nora, age ten; and Nelson, age nine.

She enjoys teaching different art techniques to them and they are very proud to watch her illustrate books.

CPSIA information can be obtained
at www.ICGtesting.com
Printed in the USA
LVIC06n2130010915
452454LV00002B/2